Cook's Chief American Office

Cook's American Tourist Tickets over 1,000 Routes, at

reduced Rates

Cook's Chief American Office

Cook's American Tourist Tickets over 1,000 Routes, at reduced Rates

ISBN/EAN: 9783337147662

Printed in Europe, USA, Canada, Australia, Japan

Cover: Foto ©ninafisch / pixelio.de

More available books at **www.hansebooks.com**

COOK'S TOURS TO VIRGINIA,

Embracing Philadelphia, Baltimore, Chesapeake Bay, James River, York River, Natural Bridge, Virginia Springs and Watering Places, Washington City, &c.

TOURS BY THE CHESAPEAKE BAY.

ROUTE 600.—NEW YORK TO RICHMOND and return, *via* Philadelphia, Wilmington, Baltimore, steamer down Chesapeake Bay (sailing at 4 P.M.), to Fortress Monroe, Norfolk, connecting with steamer on James River, to City Point, RICHMOND, thence by rail to Gordonsville, Culpepper, Alexandria, Washington City, Baltimore, Philadelphia, and New York, or *vice versa*.

First class $23.95

ROUTE 601.—NEW YORK TO RICHMOND and return, *via* rail to Philadelphia, Baltimore, steamer down Chesapeake Bay to Fortress Monroe, West Point, Fair Oaks, RICHMOND, Fredericksburg, Quantico, steamer on Potomac River to Washington City, rail to Baltimore, Philadelphia, and New York, or *vice versa*.

First class $20.15

ROUTE 602.—NEW YORK TO RICHMOND and return, *via* Philadelphia, Wilmington, Baltimore, steamer down Chesapeake Bay to Fortress Monroe, West Point, thence rail to Tunstalls, Fair Oaks, RICHMOND, Gordonsville, Orange, Culpepper, Manassas, Fairfax, Washington City, Baltimore, Philadelphia, and back to New York, or *vice versa*.

First class $20.60

ROUTE 603.—NEW YORK TO CHRISTIANSBURG (YELLOW SULPHUR SPRINGS) and return, *via* Philadelphia, Baltimore, steamer down Chesapeake Bay, to Fortress Monroe, Norfolk, rail to Petersburg, Burkeville, Lynchburg, Bonsacks, BigLick, Alleghany, Big Tunnel, CHRISTIANSBURG, returning to Lynchburg, Charlotteville, Gordonsville, Manassas, Alexandria, Washington City, Baltimore, Philadelphia, and New York, or *vice versa*.

First class $33.05

ROUTE 604.—NEW YORK TO CHRISTIANSBURG (YELLOW SULPHUR SPRINGS) and return, *via* Philadelphia, Baltimore, steamer down Chesapeake Bay, to Fortress Monroe, Norfolk, connecting with steamer on James River, to City Point, Richmond, rail to Burkeville, Lynchburg, Bonsacks (for Natural Bridge), Alleghany, Big Tunnel, CHRISTIANSBURG, and back to Lynchburg and Richmond, thence to Gordonsville, Culpepper, Manassas, Alexandria, Washington City, Baltimore, Philadelphia, and New York, or *vice versa*.

First class $36.65

ROUTE 605.—NEW YORK TO CHRISTIANSBURG (YELLOW SULPHUR SPRINGS) and return, *via* Philadelphia, Baltimore, down Chesapeake Bay, to Fortress Monroe, Norfolk, rail to Petersburg, Burkeville, Lynchburg, Bonsacks (for Natural Bridge), Alleghany, Big Tunnel, CHRISTIANSBURG, returning to Burkeville, Richmond, Orange, Gordonsville, Manassas, Alexandria, Washington City, Baltimore, Philadelphia, and New York, or *vice versa*.

First class $36.80

ROUTE 606.—NEW YORK TO CHRISTIANSBURG (YELLOW SULPHUR SPRINGS) and return, *via* same route as above to Richmond, thence to West Point, and steamer up Chesapeake Bay to Fortress Monroe, Baltimore, rail to Philadelphia and New York, or *vice versa*.

First class $33.30

ROUTE 607.—NEW YORK TO NATURAL BRIDGE and return, *via* rail to Philadelphia, Wilmington, Baltimore, steamer down Chesapeake Bay to Fortress Monroe, Norfolk, rail to Petersburg, Burkeville, Bonsacks, stage to NATURAL BRIDGE, Lexington, Rockbridge Baths, Goshen, rail to Staunton, Harrisonburg, Strasburg, Winchester, Harper's Ferry, Washington City, Baltimore, Philadelphia and New York, or *vice versa*.

First class $34.90

ROUTE 608.—NEW YORK TO NATURAL BRIDGE and return, *via* rail to Philadelphia, Baltimore, steamer down Chesapeake Bay to Fortress Monroe, Norfolk, changing to James River steamer to City Point, Richmond, rail to Burkeville, Lynchburg, Bonsacks, stage to Natural Bridge, Lexington, Rockbridge Baths, Goshen, rail to Staunton, Charlottesville, Gordonsville, Alexandria, Washington City, Baltimore, Philadelphia and New York, or *vice versa*.

First class $37.05

ROUTE 609.—NEW YORK TO NATURAL BRIDGE and return, *via* rail to Philadelphia, Wilmington, Baltimore, steamer down the Chesapeake Bay to Fortress Monroe, Norfolk, rail to Petersburg, Burkeville, Lynchburg, Bonsacks, stage to NATURAL BRIDGE, Lexington, Rockbridge Baths, Goshen, rail to Staunton, Charlottesville, Gordonsville, Culpepper, Manassas, Alexandria, Washington City, Baltimore, Philadelphia and New York, or *vice versa*.

First class $37.20

ROUTE 610.—NEW YORK TO NATURAL BRIDGE and return, *via* rail to Philadelphia, Wilmington, Baltimore, steamer down Chesapeake Bay to Fortress Monroe, Norfolk, changing to steamer on James River to City Point, Richmond, rail to Burkeville, Lynchburg, Bonsacks, stage to NATURAL BRIDGE, Lexington, Rockbridge Baths, Goshen, rail to Staunton, Harrisonburg, Strasburg, Winchester, Harper's Ferry, Washington City, Baltimore, Philadelphia and New York, or *vice versa*.

First class $34.75

ROUTE 611.—NEW YORK TO RICHMOND, NATURAL BRIDGE, WEYER'S CAVE and return, *via* Philadelphia, Wilmington, Baltimore, then steamer down Chesapeake Bay to Fortress Monroe, West Point, rail to RICHMOND, Burkeville, Lynchburg, Bonsacks, stage to NATURAL BRIDGE, Lexington, Rockbridge Baths, Goshen, rail to Staunton, Mount Sydney, stage to Weyer's Cave, and back to Mount Sydney, rail to Harrisonburg, Strasburg, Winchester, Harper's Ferry, Point of Rocks, Washington City, Baltimore, Philadelphia, and back to New York, or *vice versa*.

First class $33.90

ROUTE 612.—NEW YORK TO CHRISTIANSBURG (Yellow Sulphur Springs) and return, *via* Philadelphia, Wilmington, Baltimore, Washington City, Manassas Gordonsville, Charlottesville, Lynchburg, Liberty, Bonsacks, Big Lick, Alleghany, Big Tunnel, CHRISTIANSBURG, returning *via* Lynchburg, Richmond, West Point, steamer on York River and Chesapeake Bay to Fortress Monroe, Baltimore, and thence rail to Philadelphia, and back to New York, or *vice versa*.

First class $20.55

ROUTE 613.—NEW YORK TO NATURAL BRIDGE and return, *via* Philadelphia, Wilmington, and Baltimore, Washington City, Point of Rocks, Harper's Ferry, Winchester, Strasburg, Harrisonburg, Staunton, Goshen, stage to Rockbridge Baths, Lexington, NATURAL BRIDGE, Bonsacks, rail to Lynchburg, Burkeville, Richmond, Fair Oaks, West Point, steamer on York River and Chesapeake Bay to Fortress Monroe, Baltimore, thence rail back to New York, or *vice versa*.

First class $31.40

ROUTE 614.—NEW YORK TO WHITE SULPHUR SPRINGS and return, *via* Philadelphia, Baltimore, down Chesapeake Bay to Fortress Monroe, York River, thence rail to Richmond, Gordonsville, Staunton, Goshen, WHITE SUL-

PHUR SPRINGS, and back to Staunton, Mount Sydney, Harrisonburg, Strasburg, Front Royal, Alexandria, Washington City, Baltimore, Philadelphia, and back to New York, or *vice versa*.

First class $30.35

ROUTE 615.—NEW YORK TO WHITE SULPHUR SPRINGS and return, *via* Philadelphia, Baltimore, Washington, Harper's Ferry, Winchester, Strasburg, Harrisonburg, Mount Sydney, Staunton, Goshen, WHITE SULPHUR SPRINGS, and back to Charlotteville, Gordonsville, Richmond, Fair Oaks, West Point, steamer up Chesapeake Bay to Fortress Monroe, Baltimore, rail to Philadelphia, and back to New York, or *vice versa*.

First class $28.70

ROUTE 616.—NEW YORK TO RICHMOND, WHITE SULPHUR SPRINGS and return, *via* rail to Philadelphia, Wilmington, Baltimore, steamer down Chesapeake Bay to Fortress Monroe, Norfolk, changing to steamer on James River to City Point, RICHMOND, and rail to Orange, Gordonsville, Charlotteville, Staunton, Goshen (for Natural Bridge), WHITE SULPHUR SPRINGS, returning to Gordonsville, Alexandria, Washington City, Baltimore, Philadelphia, and New York, or *vice versa*.

First class $34.35

ROUTE 617.—NEW YORK TO NATURAL BRIDGE, WHITE SULPHUR SPRINGS, and return, *via* rail to Philadelphia, Wilmington, Baltimore, steamer down Chesapeake Bay to Fortress Monroe, Norfolk, rail to Petersburg, Burkeville, Lynchburg, Bonsacks, stage to NATURAL BRIDGE, Lexington, Rockbridge, Bath, Goshen, rail to WHITE SULPHUR SPRINGS, returning to New York same as above, or *vice versa*.

First class $41.10

ROUTE 619.—NEW YORK TO WHITE SULPHUR SPRINGS and return, *via* rail to Philadelphia, Baltimore, steamer down Chesapeake Bay to Fortress Monroe, Norfolk, changing to steamer on James River for City Point, Richmond, rail to Orange, Gordonsville, Charlotteville, Staunton, Goshen (for Natural Bridge), WHITE SULPHUR SPRINGS, returning to Staunton, Harrisonburg, Strasburg, Winchester, Harper's Ferry, Washington City, Baltimore, Philadelphia, and New York, or *vice versa*.

First class $32.95

TOURS BY SEA TO FORTRESS MONROE.

ROUTE 620.—NEW YORK TO RICHMOND and return, *via* Old Dominion Steamship Co. steamers, sailing from Pier 37 N. R. every Tuesday, Thursday and Saturday at 3 P. M. (meals and staterooms included), to Fortress Monroe, Norfolk, RICHMOND, rail to Gordonsville, Alexandria, Washington City, Baltimore, Philadelphia, and New York, or *vice versa*.

First class $22.00

ROUTE 621.—NEW YORK TO RICHMOND and return, *via* Old Dominion Steamship Co. to Fortress Monroe, Norfolk, RICHMOND, rail to Fredericksburg, Quantico, steamer on Potomac to Washington City, Baltimore, Philadelphia, and New York, or *vice versa*.

First class $21.55

ROUTE 622.—NEW YORK TO CHRISTIANSBURG and return, *via* Old Dominion Steamship Co. to Fortress Monroe, Norfolk, Richmond, rail to Burkeville, Lynchburg, Bonsack's, CARISTIANSBURG, returning to Lynchburg, Gordonsville, Alexandria, Washington, Baltimore, Philadelphia, and New York, or *vice versa*.

First class $30.95

ROUTE 623.—NEW YORK TO CHRISTIANSBURG and return, *via* Old Dominion Steamship Co. to Fortress Monroe, Norfolk, rail to Petersburg,

Burkeville, Lynchburg, Bonsack's, CHRISTIANSBURG, Lynchburg, Gordonsville, Alexandria, Washington, Baltimore, Philadelphia, and New York, or *vice versa*.
First class $31.10

ROUTE 624.—NEW YORK TO CHRISTIANSBURG and return, *via* Old Dominion Steamship Co. to Fortress Monroe, Norfolk, rail to Petersburg, Burkeville, Lynchburg, Bonsack's, CHRISTIANSBURG, Lynchburg, Burkeville, Richmond, Quantico, steamer on Potomac to Washington, rail to Baltimore, Philadelphia, and New York, or *vice versa*.
First class $34.85

ROUTE 625.—NEW YORK TO CHRISTIANSBURG and return, *via* Old Dominion Steamship Co. to Fortress Monroe, Norfolk, rail to Petersburg, Burkeville, Lynchburg, Bonsacks, CHRISTIANSBURG, Lynchburg, Burkeville, Richmond, Gordonsville, Alexandria, Washington, Baltimore, Philadelphia, and New York, or *vice versa*.
First class $34.85

ROUTE 626.—NEW YORK TO CHRISTIANSBURG and return, *via* Old Dominion Steamship Co. to Fortress Monroe, Norfolk, rail to Petersburg, Lynchburg, Bonsacks, CHRISTIANSBURG, Lynchburg, Burkeville, Richmond, and Old Dominion Steamer (leaving every Sunday, Tuesday and Friday) direct to New York, or *vice versa*.
First class $32.60

ROUTE 627.—NEW YORK TO WHITE SULPHUR SPRINGS and return, *via* Old Dominion Steamspip Co. to Fortress Monroe, Norfolk, Richmond, rail to Gordonville, Staunton, Goshen (for Natural Bridge), WHITE SULPHUR SPRINGS, Staunton, Charlottesville, Gordonsville, Alexandria, Washington, Baltimore, Philadelphia, and New York, or *vice versa*.
First class $33.20

ROUTE 628.—NEW YORK TO WHITE SULPHUR SPRINGS and return, *via* Old Dominion Steamship Co. to Fortress Monroe, Norfolk, Richmond, rail to Gordonsville, Staunton, Goshen (for Natural Bridge), WHITE SULPHUR SPRINGS, Staunton, Strasburg, Front Royal, Washington City, Baltimore, Philadelphia, and New York, or *vice versa*
First class $32.55

ROUTE 629.—NEW YORK TO WHITE SULPHUR SPRINGS and return, *via* Old Dominion Steamship Co. to Fortress Monroe, Norfolk, Richmond, rail to Gordonsville, Staunton, Goshen (for Natural Bridge), WHITE SULPHUR SPRINGS, Staunton, Strasburg, Harper's Ferry, Washington City, Baltimore, Philadelphia, and New York, or *vice versa*.
First class $30.95

ALL RAIL TOURS.

ROUTE 630.—NEW YORK TO WASHINGTON, STRASBURG, and return, *via* rail to Philadelphia, Wilmington, Baltimore, WASHINGTON City, Alexandria, Manasses, STRASBURG, Winchester, Harper's Ferry, Point of Rocks, Baltimore, Philadelphia, Baltimore, and New York, or *vice versa*.
First class $17.50

ROUTE 631.—NEW YORK TO CHRISTIANSBURG (YELLOW SULPHUR SPRINGS) and return, *via* rail to Philadelphia, Baltimore, Washington City, Alexandria, Gordonsville, Lynchburg, Bonsacks (for Natural Bridge), Alleghany, Big Tunnel, CHRISTIANSBURG, returning to Lynchburg, Burkeville, Richmond, Fredericksburg, Quantico, steamer on Potomac River tó Washington, rail to Baltimore, Philadelphia, and New York, or *vice versa*.
First class $32.60

ROUTE 632.—NEW YORK TO CHRISTIANSBURG and return, *via* rail to Philadelphia, Baltimore, Washington City, steamer down Potomac to

Quantico, rail to Fredericksburg, Richmond, Burkeville, Lynchburg, Bonsacks, Big Tunnel, CHRISTIANSBURG, to Lynchburg, Gordonsville, Alexandria, Washington City, Baltimore, Philadelphia, and New York, or *vice versa*.

First class $32.60

ROUTE C33.—NEW YORK TO CHRISTIANSBURG (Yellow Sulphur Springs) and return, *via* Philadelphia, Wilmington, Baltimore, steamer down Chesapeake Bay to Fortress Monroe, West Point, thence rail to Fair Oaks, Richmond, Burkeville, Lynchburg, Bonsacks, Big Lick, Alleghany, Big Tunnel, CHRISTIANSBURG, returning to Lynchburg, Burkeville, Richmond, Gordonsville, Orange, Culpepper, Manassas, Alexandria, Washington, Baltimore, Philadelphia, and back to New York, or *vice versa*.

First class $33.30

ROUTE 634.—NEW YORK TO CHRISTIANSBURG (Yellow Sulphur Springs) and return, *via* Philadelphia, Baltimore, Washington City, Mannasses, Gordonsville, Charlottesville, Lynchburg, Bonsacks, Big Lick, Alleghany, Big Tunnel, Christiansburg, returning to New York the same way.

First class $29.30

ROUTE 635.—NEW YORK TO CHRISTIANSBURG (Yellow Sulphur Springs) and return, *via* Philadelphia, Baltimore, Washington City, Alexandria, Manasses, Gordonsville, Charlottesville, Lynchburg, Liberty, Bonsacks, Big Lick, Alleghany, Big Tunnel, CHRISTIANSBURG, *via* Lynchburg, Burkeville, Richmond, Gordonsville, Washington, Baltimore and Philadelphia, or *vice versa*.

First class $33.00

ROUTE 636.—NEW YORK TO NATURAL BRIDGE, Virginia, and return, *via* Philadelphia, Baltimore, Washington City, Gordonsville, Staunton, Goshen, thence by stage to Rockbridge Baths, Lexington, NATURAL BRIDGE, returning same way.

First class $33.30

ROUTE 637.—NEW YORK TO NATURAL BRIDGE and return, *via* rail to Philadelphia, Baltimore, Washington City, steamer down the Potomac to Quantico, rail to Fredericksburg, Richmond, Burkeville, Lynchburg, Bonsacks, stage to Natural Bridge, Lexington, Goshen, and rail to Staunton, Gordonsville, Alexandria, Washington City, Baltimore, Philadelphia and New York, or *vice versa*.

First class $36.75

ROUTE 638.—NEW YORK TO NATURAL BRIDGE and return, *via* Philadelphia, Baltimore, Washington City, Manassas, Gordonsville, Staunton, Goshen, stage to Rockbridge Baths, Lexington, NATURAL BRIDGE, Bonsacks, rail to Lynchburg, Charlottesville, Gordonsville, Washington, Baltimore, and back to New York, or *vice versa*.

First class $33.45

ROUTE 639.—NEW YORK TO NATURAL BRIDGE and return, same as above to Lynchburg, thence to Burkeville, Richmond, Fair Oaks, West Point, and steamer on York River and Chesapeake Bay to Fortress Monroe, Baltimore, thence to New York, or *vice versa*.

First class $33.70

ROUTE 640.—NEW YORK TO NATURAL BRIDGE and return, *via* Philadelphia, Baltimore, Washington City, Manassas, Culpepper, Gordonsville, Richmond, Burkeville, Lynchburg, Bonsacks, thence stage to Natural Bridge, Lexington, Rockbridge Baths, Goshen, and rail to Staunton, Gordonsville, Washington, Baltimore, and back to New York, or *vice versa*.

First class $37.20

ROUTE 641.—NEW YORK TO NATURAL BRIDGE and return, *via* Philadelphia, Wilmington, Baltimore, Washington City, Harper's Ferry, Winchester, Strasburg, Staunton, Goshen, and stage to Rockbridge Baths, Lexington, Natural Bridge, and back the same way.

First class $28.25

ROUTE 642.—NEW YORK TO NATURAL BRIDGE and return, *via* Philadelphia, Wilmington, Baltimore, Washington City, Harper's Ferry, Winchester, Strasburg, Harisonburg, Staunton, Goshen, stage to Rockbridge Baths, Lexington, NATURAL BRIDGE, and back to Goshen, thence rail to Gordonsville, Manassas, Alexandria, Washington, Baltimore, Philadelphia and New York, or *vice versa*.
First class $31.00

ROUTE 643.—NEW YORK TO NATURAL BRIDGE and return, *via* Philadelphia, Wilmington, Baltimore, Washington City, Harper's Ferry, Winchester, Strasburg, Harrisonburg, Staunton, Goshen, stage to Lexington, Natural Bridge, Bonsacks, rail to Lynchburg, Burkeville, Richmond, Gordonsville, Culpepper, Manassas, Alexandria, Washington, Baltimore, Philadelphia, and back to New York, or *vice versa*.
First class $34.95

ROUTE 644.—NEW YORK TO NATURAL BRIDGE and return, *via* Philadelphia, Baltimore, Washington City, Harper's Ferry, Winchester, Strasburg, Staunton, Goshen, stage to Lexington, NATURAL BRIDGE, Bonsacks, rail to Lynchburg, Burkeville, Richmond, Fredericksburg, Quantico, steamer on Potomac to Washington City, rail to Baltimore, Philadelphia, and New York, or *vice versa*.
First class $34.45

ROUE 645.—NEW YORK TO NATURAL BRIDGE and return, *via* Philadelphia, Baltimore, Washington City, Alexandria, Gordonsville, Charlottesville, Staunton, Goshen, stage to Rockbridge Baths, Lexington. NATURAL BRIDGE, Bonsacks, rail to Lynchburg, Burkeville, Richmond, Fredericksburg, Quantico, steamer on Potomac to Washington, Baltimore, Philadelphia, and New York.
First class $36.75

ROUTE 646.—NEW YORK TO NATURAL BRIDGE and return, *via* Philadelphia, Wilmington, Baltimore, Washington, Point of Rocks, Harper's Ferry, Winchester, Strasburg, Harrisonburg, Staunton, Goshen, stage to Rockbridge Baths, Lexington, NATURAL BRIDGE, Bonsacks, rail to Lynchburg, Charlottesville, Gordonsville, Culpepper, Manasses, Alexandria, Washington, Baltimore, Philadelphia, and back to New York, or *vice versa*.
First class $31.15

ROUTE 647.—NEW YORK TO NATURAL BRIDGE and return, *via* Philadelphia, Baltimore, Washington City, Alexandria, Manasses Junction, Front Royal, Strasburg, Harrisonburg, Staunton, Goshen, stage to Rockbridge Baths, Lexington, NATURAL BRIDGE, and back to Goshen, thence rail to Charlottesville, Gordonsville, Alexandria, Washington, Baltimore, and back to New York, or *vice versa*.
First class $33.05

ROUTE 648.—NEW YORK TO NATURAL BRIDGE and return, *via* Philadelphia, Baltimore, Washington, Alexandria, Manassas, Front Royal, Strasburg, Harrisonburg, Staunton, Goshen, stage to Rockbridge Baths, Lexington, NATURAL BRIDGE, and back to Goshen, thence rail to Staunton, Strasburg, Winchester, Harper's Ferry, Baltimore, Philadelphia, and back to New York, or *vice versa*.
First class $30.35

ROUTE 649.—NEW YORK TO WEYER'S CAVE and return, *via* Philadelphia, Wilmington, Baltimore, Washington, Point of Rocks, Harper's Ferry, Winchester, Harrisonburg, Mount Sydney, stage to Weyer's Cave, thence rail to Staunton, Charlottesville, Gordonsville, Manasses, Alexandria, Washington, Baltimore, Philadelphia, and New York, or *vice versa*.
First class $23.60

ROUTE 650.—NEW YORK TO WEYER'S CAVE and return, *via* Philadel-

phia, Baltimore, Washington, Alexandria, Manasses Junction, Strasburg, Harrisonburg, Mount Sydney, stage to Cave, and back to Mount Sydney, thence rail to Staunton, Charlottesville, Gordonsville, Culpepper, Alexandria, Washington City, Baltimore, Philadelphia, and back to New York, or *vice versa*.
First class $25.25

ROUTE 651.—NEW YORK TO WEYER'S CAVE, NATURAL BRIDGE, RICHMOND and return, *via* Philadelphia, Baltimore, Washington City, Point of Rocks, Harper's Ferry, Winchester, Strasburg, Harrisonburg, Mount Sydney, stage to WEYER'S CAVE, and back to Mount Sydney, rail to Staunton, Goshen, stage to Rockbridge Baths, Lexington, NATURAL BRIDGE, Bonsacks, rail to Lynchburg, Burkeville, RICHMOND, Gordonsville, Culpepper, Manasses, Alexandria, Washington, Baltimore, Philadelphia, and back to New York, or *vice versa*.
First class $37.40

ROUTE 652.—NEW YORK TO BERKELEY SPRINGS (Va.) and return, *via* Philadelphia, Baltimore, Washington City, Point of Rocks, Sir John's Run, stage to Berkeley Springs, returning same way.
First class $17.70

ROUTE 653.—NEW YORK TO WHITE SULPHUR SPRINGS and return, *via* Philadelphia, Baltimore, Washington City, Alexandria, Manasses, Gordonsville, Staunton, Goshen, Covington, WHITE SULPHUR SPRINGS, and back the same way.
First class $29.50

ROUTE 654.—NEW YORK TO WHITE SULPHUR SPRINGS and return, *via* Philadelphia, Baltimore, Washington, Point of Rocks, Harper's Ferry, Winchester, Strasburg, Harrisonburg, Mount Sydney, Staunton, Goshen, WHITE SULPHUR SPRINGS, returning to Charlotteville, Gordonsville, Culpepper, Manassas, Alexandria Washington, Baltimore, Philadelphia, and back to New York, or *vice versa*.
First class $27.20

ROUTE 655.—NEW YORK TO WHITE SULPHUR SPRINGS and return, *via* Philadelphia, Baltimore, Washington City, Harper's Ferry, Winchester, Strasburg, Staunton, Goshen (for Natural Bridge), WHITE SULPHUR SPRINGS, returning to Goshen, Staunton, Charlotteville, Gordonsville, Richmond, Fredericksburg, Quantico, steamer on Potomac to Washington City, rail to Baltimore, Philadelphia, and back to New York, or *vice versa*.
First class $31.75

ROUTE 656.—NEW YORK TO WHITE SULPHUR SPRINGS and return, *via* Philadelphia, Wilmington, Baltimore, Washington, Point of Rocks, Harper's Ferry, Winchester, Staunton, Goshen, Covington, WHITE SULPHUR SPRINGS, and back the same way.
First class $24.95

ROUTE 657.—NEW YORK TO OAKLAND and return, *via* Philadelphia, Baltimore, Washington City, Point of Rocks, Harper's Ferry, Cumberland, OAKLAND, and return the same way.
First class $20.05

ROUTE 658.—NEW YORK TO DEER PARK and return, *via* Philadelphia, Wilmington, Baltimore, Washington, Point of Rocks, Harper's Ferry, Cumberland, DEER PARK, and back the same way.
First class $19.80

TOURS TO WEST VIRGINIA.

ROUTE 659.—NEW YORK TO WEST VIRGINIA, OHIO RIVER, and return, *via* Philadelphia, Baltimore, Washington City, Point of Rocks, Harper's Ferry, Grafton, Parkersburg, Hamden, Portsmouth, steamer on Ohio River, to Huntington, thence rail to Kanawha Falls, White Sulphur Springs, Coving-

ton, Goshen, Staunton, Charlotteville, Gordonsville, Manassas Junction, Alexandria, Washington, Baltimore, Philadelphia, New York, or *vice versa*.
First class $34.15

ROUTE 660.—NEW YORK TO WEST VIRGINIA, OHIO RIVER, and return, *via* Philadelphia, Baltimore, Washington City, Point of Rocks, Harper's Ferry, Winchester, Harrisonburg, Staunton, Goshen, White Sulphur Springs, Kanawha, Huntington, steamer on Ohio River to Portsmouth, rail to Hamden, Parkersburg, Grafton, Cumberland, Sir John's Run, Baltimore, Philadelphia, New York, or *vice versa*.
First class $33.65

ROUTE 661.—NEW YORK TO RICHMOND, WEST VIRGINIA, OHIO RIVER, and return, *via* Philadelphia, Baltimore, steamer down Chesapeake Bay to Fortress Monroe, West Point, thence rail to Fair Oaks, RICHMOND, Gordonsville, Charlotteville, Staunton, Goshen, White Sulphur Springs, Kanawha, Huntington, down Ohio River to Portsmouth, thence rail to Hamden, Parkersburg, Grafton, Cumberland, Harper's Ferry, Point of Rocks, Washington City, Baltimore, Philadelphia, New York, or *vice versa*.
First class $34.80

ROUTE 662.—NEW YORK TO WEST VIRGINIA, RICHMOND, and return, *via* Philadelphia, Baltimore, Washington City, Harper's Ferry, Cumberland, Grafton, Parkersburg, Hamden, Portsmouth, steamer on Ohio River to Huntington, rail to Kanawha, White Sulphur Springs, Goshen, Staunton, Charotteville, RICHMOND, Gordonsville, Culpepper, Manassas, Alexandria, Washington, Baltimore, Philadelphia, New York, or *vice versa*.
First class $33.30

ROUTE 663.—NEW YORK TO RICHMOND, WEST VIRGINIA, and return, *via* rail to Philadelphia, Baltimore, steamer down Chesapeake Bay to Fortress Monroe, Norfolk, changing to steamer on James River to City Point, Richmond, rail to Orange, Charlotteville, Staunton, Goshen (for Natural Bridge), White Sulphur Springs, Kanawha, Huntington; steamer down the Ohio River to Portsmouth, rail to Hamden, Parkersburg, Grafton, Cumberland, Harper's Ferry, Washington City, Baltimore, Philadelphia, and New York, or *vice versa*.
First class $38.25

ROUTE 664.—NEW YORK TO RICHMOND, WEST VIRGINIA, and return, *via* rail to Philadelphia, Baltimore, Washington City, steamer on Potomac, to Quantico, rail to Fredericksburg, RICHMOND, Orange, Gordonsville, Charlotteville, Staunton, Strasburg, Winchester, Harper's Ferry, Point of Rocks, Washington, Baltimore, Philadelphia, and New York, or *vice versa*.
First class $24.65

ROUTE 665.—NEW YORK TO RICHMOND, WEST VIRGINIA, and return, *via* rail to Philadelphia, Baltimore, Washington City, steamer down Potomac to Quantico, rail to Fredericksburg, RICHMOND, Gordonsville, Charlottesville, Staunton, Goshen (for Natural Bridge), White Sulphur Springs, Kanawha, Huntington, steamer on Ohio River to Portsmouth, Hamden, Parkersburg, Grafton, Cumberland, Harper's Ferry, Washington City, Baltimore, Philadelphia and New York, or *vice versa*.
First class $37.85

ROUTE 666.—NEW YORK TO RICHMOND, WEST VIRGINIA, and return, *via* Old Dominion Steamship Co. to Fortress Monroe, Norfolk, RICHMOND, rail to Gordonville, Charlottesville, Staunton, Harrisonburg, Strasburg, Front Royal, Washington City, Baltimore, Philadelphia, and New York, or *vice versa*.
First class $25.65

ROUTE 667.—NEW YORK TO RICHMOND, WEST VIRGINIA and return, *via* Old Dominion Steamship Co. to Fortress Monroe, Norfolk, RICHMOND,

rail to Gordonsville, Charlottesville, Staunton, Strasburg, Harper's Ferry, Washington City, Baltimore, Philadelphia, and New York, or *vice versa*.
First class $24.00
Route 668.—NEW YORK TO RICHMOND, WEST VIRGINIA and return, *via* Old Dominion Steamship Co. to Fortress Monroe, Norfolk, Richmond, rail to Gordonsville, Charlottesville, Staunton, Goshen (for Natural Bridge), White Sulphur Springs, Huntington, steamer on Ohio River to Portsmouth, rail to Hamden, Parkersburg, Cumberland, Harper's Ferry, Washington, Baltimore, Philadelphia, and New York, or *vice versa*.
First class $41.55

TOURS TO THE SOUTH,

BY RAIL FROM NEW YORK.

Route 669.—NEW YORK TO ATLANTA and return, *via* rail to Philadelphia, Baltimore, Washington City, steamer on Potomac to Quantico, rail to Fredericksburg, Richmond, Burkeville, Greensboro, Charlotte, Spartansburg, Greenville, ATLANTA, Kingston, Dalton, Cleveland, Knoxville, Bristol, Wytheville, Christiansburg, Bonsacks, Lynchburgh, Charlottesville, Gordonsville, Alexandria, Washington City, Baltimore, Philadelphia and New York, or *vice versa*.
First class $57.70
Route 670.—NEW YORK TO ATLANTA and return, *via* Philadelphia, Baltimore, steamer down Chesapeake Bay to Fortress Monroe, West Point, thence rail to Burkeville, Danville, Greensboro, Charlotte, Spartansburg, Greenville. ATLANTA. Kingston, Resaca, Dalton, Cleveland, Knoxville, Bristol, Glade Springs, Wytheville, Christiansburg, Bonsacks (for Natural Bridge), Lynchburg, Gordonsville, Culpepper, Manassas, Alexandria, Washington City, Baltimore, Philadelphia, New York, or *vice versa*.
First class $56.65
Route 671.—NEW YORK TO ATLANTA and return, *via* Philadelphia, Baltimore, Washington, Alexandria, Manassas, Culpepper, Gordonsville, Lynchburg, Bonsacks (for Natural Bridge), Christiansburg (Greenbrier White Sulphur Springs), Wytheville, Glade Springs, Bristol, Knoxville, Cleveland, Dalton, Kingston, Resaca, Atlanta, Greenville, Spartansburg, Charlotte, Greensboro, Danville, Burkeville, Richmond, Gordonsville, Alexandria, Washington. Baltimore, Philadelphia, New York, or *vice versa*.
First class $58.15
Route 672.—NEW YORK TO WILMINGTON, CHARLESTON, and return, *via* rail to Philadelphia, Baltimore, steamer down Chesapeake Bay to Fortress Monroe, Norfolk, rail to Weldon, Goldsboro, WILMINGTON, Florence, CHARLESTON, Augusta, Columbia. Charlotte, Greensboro, Richmond, Gordonsville, Alexandria, Washington City, Baltimore, Philadelphia and New York, or *vice versa*.
First class $58.75
Route 673.—NEW YORK TO CHARLESTON and return, *via* rail to Philadelphia, Wilmington, Baltimore, Washington City, Alexandria, Gordonsville, Richmond, Greensboro, Charlotte, Augusta, CHARLESTON, Columbia, Wilmington, Goldsboro, Weldon, Norfolk, steamer up Chesapeake Bay to Fortress Monroe Baltimore, rail to Philadelphia and New York, or *vice versa*.
First class $60.30
Route 674.—NEW YORK TO CHARLESTON, ATLANTA, and return, *via* rail to Philadelphia, Baltimore, steamer down Chesapeake Bay to Fortress Monroe Norfolk, rail to Weldon, Goldsboro, Wilmington, Florence, CHARLESTON, Augusta, Charlotte, ATLANTA, Kingston, Dalton, Cleveland, Knoxville, Bristol, Glade Springs, Wytheville, Christiansburg, Bonsacks (for Natural

Bridge), Lynchburg, Gordonsville, Alexandria, Washington City, Baltimore, Philadelphia and New York, or *vice versa*.

First class **$73.85**

ROUTE 675.—NEW YORK TO CHARLESTON and return, *via* rail to Philadelphia, Baltimore, steamer down the Chesapeake Bay to Fortress Monroe, Norfolk, rail to Weldon, Goldsboro, Wilmington, Florence, CHARLESTON, Augusta, Charlotte, Greensboro, Richmond, Fredericksburg, Quantico, steamer on Potomac to Washington City, rail to Baltimore, Philadelphia and New York, or *vice versa*.

First class **$56.30**

ROUTE 676.—NEW YORK TO ATLANTA, CHARLESTON, and return, *via* rail to Philadelphia, Baltimore, Washington City, steamer on Potomac to Quantico, rail to Fredericksburg, Richmond, Burkeville, Greensboro, Charlotte, Greenville, ATLANTA, Charlotte, Augusta, CHARLESTON, Florence, Wilmington, Weldon, Norfolk, steamer on Chesapeake Bay to Baltimore, rail to Philadelphia and New York, or *vice versa*.

First class **$72.20**

ROUTE 677.—NEW YORK TO ATLANTA, CHARLESTON, and return, *via* rail to Philadelphia, Baltimore, Washington City, Alexandria, Manassas, Gordonsville, Orange, Richmond, Burkeville, Lynchburg, Bonsacks (for Natural Bridge), Christiansburg, Wytheville, Bristol, Knoxville, Cleveland, Dalton, Kingston, ATLANTA, Charlotte, Augusta, CHARLESTON, Florence, Wilmington, Goldsboro, Weldon, Norfolk, steamer on Chesapeake Bay to Fortress Monroe, Baltimore, rail to Philadelphia and New York, or *vice versa*.

First class **$77.60**

ROUTE 678.—NEW YORK TO ATLANTA, CHARLESTON, and return, *via* rail to Philadelphia, Baltimore, steamer down the Chesapeake Bay to Norfolk, rail to Petersburg, Burkeville, Lynchburg, Bonsacks (for Natural Bridge,) Christiansburg, Wytheville, Bristol, Knoxville, Cleveland, Kingston, ATLANTA, Charlotte, Augusta, CHARLESTON, Florence, Wilmington, Goldsboro, Weldon, Norfolk, steamer on Chesapeake Bay to Fortress Monroe, Baltimore, rail to Philadelphia and New York, or *vice versa*.

First class **$73.65**

TOURS TO THE SOUTH BY SEA FROM NEW YORK.

ROUTE 679:—NEW YORK TO ATLANTA and return, *via* Old Dominion Steamship Co. to Fortress Monroe, Norfolk, Richmond, Burkeville, Greensboro, Charlotte, Spartansburg, Greenville, ATLANTA, Kingston, Dalton, Cleveland, Knoxville, Bristol, Wytheville, Christiansburg, Bonsack's, Lynchburg, Charlottesville, Gordonsville, Alexandria, Washington City, Baltimore, Philadelphia, and New York, or *vice versa*.

First class **$56.10**

ROUTE 680.—NEW YORK TO ATLANTA and return, *via* Old Dominion Steamship Co. to Fortress Monroe, Norfolk, Richmond, rail to Danville, Greensboro, Charlotte, Spartansburg, Greenville, ATLANTA, returning same way to Richmond, thence Gordonsville, Alexandria, Washington, Baltimore, Philadelphia, and New York, or *vice versa*.

First class **$54.85**

ROUTE 681.—NEW YORK TO ATLANTA and return, *via* Old Dominion Steamship Co. to Fortress Monroe, Norfolk, Richmond, Danville, Greensboro, Charlotte, Greenville, ATLANTA, returning same way to Richmond, thence to Quantico, and steamer up the Potomac to Washington, rail to Baltimore, Philadelphia and New York, or *vice versa*.

First class **$54.37**

ROUTE 682.—NEW YORK TO WILMINGTON, CHARLESTON and re-

return, *via* Old Dominion Steamship Co. to Fortress Monroe, Norfolk, rail to Weldon, Goldsboro, WILMINGTON, Florence, CHARLESTON, Augusta, Columbia, Charlotte, Greensboro, Richmond, Gordonsville, Alexandria, Washington City, Baltimore, Philadelphia, and New York, or *vice versa*.

First class $54.80

ROUTE 683.—NEW YORK TO CHARLESTON and return, *via* Old Dominion Steamship Co. to Fortress Monroe, Norfolk, rail to Welden, Goldsboro, Wilmington, Florence, CHARLESTON, Augusta, Charlotte, Greensboro, Richmond, Fredericksburg, Quantico, steamer on Potomac to Washington City, rail to Baltimore, Philadelphia, and New York, or *vice versa*.

First class $54.35

ROUTE 684.—NEW YORK TO CHARLESTON and return, *via* Old Dominion Steamship Co. to Fortress Monroe, Norfolk, rail to Weldon, Goldsboro, Wilmington, Florence, CHARLESTON, Augusta, Charlotte, Greensboro, Richmond, Gordonsville, Washington, Baltimore, Philadelphia, and New York, or *vice versa*.

First class $55.80

TOURS TO THE SOUTH WEST.

ROUTE 685.—NEW YORK TO CHATTANOOGA and return, *via* Philadelphia, Wilmington, Baltimore, steamer down Chesapeake Bay to Fortress West Point, rail to Richmond, Burkeville, Lynchburg, Bonsacks, Wytheville, Bristol, Knoxville, Cleveland, CHATTANOOGA, and back same way to Lynchburg, Gordonsville, Manassas, Alexandria, Washington City, Baltimore, Philadelphia, and New York, or *vice versa*.

First class $53.00

ROUTE 686.—NEW YORK TO CHATTANOOGA and return, *via* Philadelphia, Baltimore, Washington City, Alexandria, Culpepper, Gordonsville, Charlotteville, Lynchburg, Bonsacks, Christiansburg, Wytheville. Bristol, Knoxville, CHATTANOOGA, and back to Lynchburg, Burkeville, Richmond, Gordonsville, Alexandria, Washington City, Baltimore, Philadelphia, New York, or *vice versa*.

First class $56.50

ROUTE 687.—NEW YORK TO CHATTANOOGA and return, *via* rail to Philadelphia, Baltimore, steamer down Chesapeake Bay to Fortress Monroe, Norfolk, rail to Petersburg, Burkeville, Lynchburg, Bonsacks (for Natural Bridge), Christiansburg, Wytheville, Bristol, Knoxville, Cleveland, CHATTANOOGA, and return to Lynchburg, Charlotteville, Gordonsville, Alexandria, Washington City, Baltimore, Philadelphia, and New York, or *vice versa*.

First class $56.55

ROUTE 688.—NEW YORK TO CHATTANOOGA and return, *via* same route as above, to CHATTANOOGA, returning to Burkeville, Richmond, Gordonsville, Alexandria, Washington City, Baltimore, Philadelphia, and New York, or *vice versa*.

First class $61.85

ROUTE 389.—NEW YORK TO CHATTANOOGA and return, *via* rail to Philadelphia, Baltimore, Washington City, steamer down Potomac to Quantico, rail to Fredericksburg, Richmond, Burkeville, Lynchburg, Bonsacks, Christiansburg, Bristol, Knoxville, Cleveland, CHATTANOOGA, and back same way to Lynchburg, Gordonsville, Alexandria, Washington City, Baltimore, Philadelphia, and New York, or *vice versa*.

First class $52.25

ROUTE 690.—NEW YORK TO MEMPHIS and return, *via* Philadelphia, Baltimore, Washington City, Alexandria, Gordonsville, Charlotteville, Lynchburg, Bonsacks, Christiansburg, Wytheville, Bristol, Knoxville, Cleveland,

Chattanooga, Stevenson, Decatur, Corinth, Grand Junction, MEMPHIS, and back same way to Lynchburg, Burkeville, Richmond, West Point, steamer on Chesapeake Bay to Fortress Monroe, Baltimore, Philadelphia, and back to New York, or *vice versa*.
First class $00.00

ROUTE 691.—NEW YORK TO MEMPHIS and return, *via* Philadelphia, Baltimore, Washington City, Alexandria, Gordonsville, Richmond, Greensboro, Charlotte, Atlanta, Dalton, Chattanooga (for Lookout Mountain), Stevenson, Decatur, Corinth, Grand Junction, MEMPHIS, and back same way to Chattanooga, Cleveland, Knoxville, Wytheville, Christiansburg, Bonsacks, Lynchburg, Charlotteville, Culpepper, Manassas, Alexandria, Washington, Baltimore, Philadelphia, and New York, or *vice versa*.
First class $00.00

ROUTE 692.—NEW YORK TO MEMPHIS and return, *via* rail to Philadelphia, Baltimore, steamer down the Chesapeake Bay to Fortress Monroe Norfolk, rail to Petersburg, Burkeville, Lynchburg, Bonsacks (for Natural Bridge), Christiansburg, Wytheville, Bristol, Knoxville, Cleveland, Chattanooga (for Lookout Mountain), Stevenson, Decatur, Corinth, Grand Junction, and back same way to Lynchburg, Charlotteville, Gordonsville, Alexandria, Washington City, Baltimore, Philadelphia, and New York, or *vice versa*.
First class $00.00

ROUTE 693.—NEW YORK TO MEMPHIS and return, *via* same route as above, to MEMPHIS, returning to Lynchburg, Burkeville, Richmond, Gordonsville, Alexandria, Washington City, Baltimore, Philadelphia, and New York, or *vice versa*.
First class $00.00

ROUTE 694.—NEW YORK TO CHARLESTON, MEMPHIS, and return, *via* rail to Philadelphia, Baltimore, steamer down Chesapeake Bay to Fortress Monroe, Norfolk, rail to Weldon, Goldsboro, Wilmington, Florence, CHARLESTON, Augusta, Charlotte, Atlanta, Kingston, Dalton, Chattanooga (for Lookout Mountain), Decatur, Corinth, Grand Junction, MEMPHIS, returning same way to Chattanooga, Cleveland, Knoxville, Bristol, Wytheville, Christiansburg, Bonsacks (for Natural Bridge), Lynchburg, Burkeville, Richmond, Gordonsville, Alexandria, Washington City, Baltimore, Philadelphia, and New York, or *vice versa*.
First class $00.00

ROUTE 695.—NEW YORK TO MEMPHIS, ATLANTA, CHARLESTON, and return, *via* rail to Philadelphia, Baltimore, Washington City, Alexandria, Gordonsville, Lynchburg, Bonsacks (for Natural Bridge), Christiansburg, Wytheville, Bristol, Knoxville, Cleveland, Chattanooga (for Lookout Mountain), Stevenson, Decatur, Corinth, Grand Junction, MEMPHIS, returning to Chattanooga, Dalton, Kingston, ATLANTA, Charlotte, Columbia, Augusta, CHARLESTON, Florence, Wilmington, Goldsboro, Weldon, Norfolk, steamer on Chesapeake Bay to Fortress Monroe, Baltimore, and rail to Philadelphia and New York, or *vice versa*.
First class $00.00

ROUTE 696.—NEW YORK TO MEMPHIS and return, *via* rail to Philadelphia, Baltimore, Washington City, steamer down Potomac to Quantico, rail to Fredericksburg, Richmond, Burkeville, Lynchburg, Bonsacks (for Natural Bridge), Christiansburg, Bristol, Knoxville, Cleveland, Chattanooga (for Lookout Mountain), Stevenson, Decatur, Corinth, Grand Junction, MEMPHIS, returning same way to Lynchburg, thence Charlotteville, Gordonsville, Alexandria, Washington, Baltimore, Philadelphia, and New York, or *vice versa*.
First class $00.00

ROUTE 697.—NEW YORK TO SELMA and return, *via* rail to Philadelphia, Baltimore, steamer down Chesapeake Bay to Fortress Monroe, Norfolk, rail to

Petersburg, Burkeville, Lynchburg, Bonsacks (for Natural Bridge), Christians-
burg, Wytheville, Bristol, Knoxville, Cleveland, Dalton, Rome, Calera, SELMA,
Rome, Dalton, Knoxville, Bristol, Wytheville, Christiansburg, Lynchburg, Gor-
donsville, Alexandria, Washington City, Baltimore, Philadelphia, and New
York, or *vice versa*.
First class $72.45

ROUTE 698.—NEW YORK TO SELMA and return, *via* same route as above
to SELMA, returning to Rome, Dalton, Knoxsville, Bristol, Christiansburg,
Bonsacks, Lynchburg, Burkeville, Richmond, Gordonsville, Alexandria, Washington City, Baltimore, Philadelphia, and New York.
First class $76.00

ROUTE 699.—NEW YORK TO SELMA and return, *via* rail to Philadelphia, Baltimore, Washington City, steamer on Potomac to Quantico, rail to
Richmond, Burkeville, Lynchburg, Bonsacks, Christiansburg, Bristol, Knoxville, Cleveland, Dalton, Rome, Calera, SELMA, returning the same way to
Lynchburg, thence Gordonsville, Alexandria, Washington, Baltimore, Philadelphia, and New York, or *vice versa*.
First class $71.80

ROUTE 700.—NEW YORK TO SELMA and return, *via* rail to Philadelphia,
Baltimore, steamer down Chesapeake Bay to Fortress Monroe, Norfolk, rail to
Petersburg, Burkeville, Lynchburg, Bonsacks, Christiansburg, Bristol, Knox-
ville, Cleveland, Dalton, Rome, Calera, SELMA, back same way to Burkeville,
Richmond, Fredericksburg, Quantico, steamer on Potomac to Washington City,
rail to Baltimore, Philadelphia, and New York, or *vice versa*.
First class $75.55

ROUTE 701.—NEW YORK TO SELMA and return, *via* Philadelphia, Baltimore, Washington, Alexandria, Gordonsville, Lynchburg, Bonsacks (for Natural Bridge), Christiansburg (Greenbrier White Sulphur Springs), Wytheville,
Bristol, Knoxville, Cleveland, Dalton, Rome, Calera, SELMA, Rome, Dalton,
Resaca, Kingston, Atlanta, Greenville, Spartansburg, Charlotte, Greensboro,
Danville, Burkeville, Richmond, West Point, and steamer up Chesapeake Bay
to Fortress Monroe, Baltimore, thence rail to Philadelphia and New York, or
vice versa.
First class   .   .   .   .   .   ,   . $70.25

ROUTE 702.—NEW YORK TO SELMA and return, *via* rail to Philadelphia,
Baltimore, Washington, steamer on Potomac to Quantico, rail to Richmond,
Danville, Greensboro, Charlotte, Greenville, Atlanta, West Point, Montgomery,
SELMA, Calera, Rome, Dalton, Knoxville, Bristol, Christiansburg, Bonsacks,
Lynchburg, Gordonsville, Alexandria, Washington City, Baltimore, Philadel-
phia and New York, or *vice versa*.
First class   -   -   -   -   -   - $71.65

ROUTE 703.—NEW YORK TO MONTGOMERY and return, *via* Philadel-
phia, Baltimore, Washington City, Alexandria, Gordonsville, Lynchburg, Bon-
sacks, Christiansburg, Bristol, Knoxville, Dalton, Rome, Calera, Selma, MONT-
GOMERY, West Point, Atlanta, Greenville, Charlotte, Greensboro, Burkeville,
Richmond, West Point, and steamer to Fortress Monroe, Baltimore, rail to
Philadelphia, New York, or *vice versa*.
First class   -   -   .   -   -   - $68.60

TOURS TO NEW ORLEANS,
COMBINING THE MISSISSIPPI RIVER.

ROUTE 704.—NEW YORK TO NEW ORLEANS and return, *via* rail to Philadelphia, Baltimore, Washington City, steamer to Quantico, rail to Richmond,
Greensboro, Charlotte, Atlanta, West Point, Montgomery, Mobile, NEW OR-

LEANS, steamer. On Mississippi River to Vicksburg, Memphis, Cairo, St. Louis, rail to Cincinnati, Parkersburg, Cumberland, Baltimore, Philadelphia, and New York, (meals and staterooms on Mississippi River included), or *vice versa*.
First class - - - - - - $95.85

ROUTE 705.—NEW YORK TO NEW ORLEANS and return, *via* rail to Philadelphia, Baltimore, Washington City, Gordonsville, Richmond, Greensboro, Atlanta, West Point, Montgomery, Mobile, NEW ORLEANS, steamer on Mississippi River (meals and staterooms included) to Vicksburg, Memphis, Cairo, St. Louis, rail to Chicago, Detroit, Niagara Falls, Albany, and down the Hudson by rail or boat to New York, or *vice versa*.
First class - - - - - - $95.85

ROUTE 706.—NEW YORK TO NEW ORLEANS and return, *via* rail to Philadelphia, Baltimore, Washington City, Gordonsville, Lynchburg, Bristol, Knoxville, Dalton, Atlanta, West Point, Montgomery, Mobile, NEW ORLEANS, steamer on Mississippi (meals and staterooms included) to Vicksburg, Memphis, Cairo, St. Louis, rail to Cincinnati, Parkersburg, Cumberland, Baltimore, Philadelphia, New York, or *vice versa*.
First class - - - - - - $93.95

ROUTE 707.—NEW YORK TO NEW ORLEANS and return, *via* same route as above to St. Louis, thence by rail to Chicago, Detroit, Niagara Falls, Albany, and down the Hudson (by rail or boat) to New York, or *vice versa*.
First class - - - - - - $97.00

ROUTE 708.—NEW YORK TO NEW ORLEANS and return, *via* rail to Philadelphia, Baltimore, steamer down Chesapeake Bay to Fortress Monroe, West Point, rail to Richmond, Greensboro, Charlotte, Atlanta, West Point, Montgomery, Mobile, NEW ORLEANS, steamer on Mississippi River (meals and staterooms included) to Vicksburg, Memphis, Cairo, St. Louis, rail to Cincinnati, Parkersburg, Baltimore, Philadelphia, New York, or *vice versa*.
First class - - - - - - $90.20

ROUTE 709.—NEW YORK TO NEW ORLEANS and return, *via* same route as above to St. Louis, thence rail to Chicago, Detroit, Niagara Falls, Albany, and down the Hudson (by rail or boat) to New York, or *vice versa*.
First class - - - - - - $94.30

ROUTE 710.—NEW YORK TO NEW ORLEANS and return, *via* rail to Philadelphia, Baltimore, steamer down Chesapeake Bay to Fortress Monroe, Norfolk, Petersburg, Lynchburg, Bristol, Knoxville, Dalton, Atlanta, West Point, Montgomery, Mobile, NEW ORLEANS, steamer up Mississippi River (meals and staterooms included) to Vicksburg, Memphis, Cairo, St. Louis, rail to Cincinnati, Parkersburg, Cumberland, Baltimore, Philadelphia, and New York, or *vice versa*.
First class - - - - - - $97.70

ROUTE 711.—NEW YORK TO NEW ORLEANS and return, *via* same route as above to St. Louis, thence rail to Chicago, Detroit, Niagara Falls, Albany, and down the Hudson (by rail or boat) to New York, or *vice versa*.
First class - - - - - - $100.00

ROUTE 712.—NEW YORK TO NEW ORLEANS and return, *via* Philadelphia, Baltimore, steamer down Chesapeake Bay to Fortress Monroe, Norfolk, rail to Weldon, Wilmington, Florence, Charleston, Augusta, Columbia, Charlotte, Atlanta, West Point, Montgomery, Mobile, NEW ORLEANS, and steamer on Mississippi River (meals and staterooms included) to Vicksburg, Memphis, Cairo, St. Louis, rail to Cincinnati, Parkersburg, Baltimore, Philadelphia, New York, or *vice versa*.
First class - - - - - - $109.40

ROUTE 713.—NEW YORK TO NEW ORLEANS and return, *via* same route as above to St. Louis, rail to Chicago, Detroit, Niagara Falls, Albany, and down the Hudson (by rail or boat) to New York, or *vibe versa*.
First class - - - - - - $111.50

TOURS TO THE WEST,

VIA PHILADELPHIA.

ROUTE 714.—NEW YORK TO CINCINNATI and return, via Philadelphia, Baltimore, Washington, Harper's Ferry, Cumberland, Parkersburg, Chillicothe, CINCINNATI, thence by steamer up the Ohio River to Huntington, rail to Kanawha, White Sulphur Springs, Goshen, Staunton, Gordonsville, Manassas, Alexandria, Washington, Baltimore, Philadelphia, and New York, or vice versa.
First class $36.70

ROUTE 715.—NEW YORK TO RICHMOND, CINCINNATI, and return, via Philadelphia, Baltimore, steamer down Chesapeake Bay to Fortress Monroe, West Point, rail to Richmond, Gordonsville, Charlotteville, Staunton, White Sulphur Springs, Huntington, and steamer down Ohio River to CINCINNATI, returning by rail to Chillicothe, Parkersburg, Grafton, Cumberland, Harper's Ferry, Washington City, Baltimore, Philadelphia, and New York, or vice versa.
• First class . . . . , . $37.35

ROUTE 716.—NEW YORK TO CINCINNATI and return, via Philadelphia, Harrisburg, Altoona, Pittsburg, Steubenville, Newark, Columbus, Xenia, CINCINNATI, and back by rail to Chillicothe, Parkersburg, Grafton, Cumberland, Harper's Ferry, Washington City, Baltimore, Philadelphia, and New York.
First class $33.55

ROUTE 717.—NEW YORK TO CINCINNATI and return, via Philadelphia-Harrisburg, Altoona, Pittsburg, Steubenville, Newark, Columbus, Xenia, Cincinnati, and back by steamer on Ohio River to Huntington, Kanawha, Alleghany Mountains, White Sulphur Springs, Staunton, Charlotteville, Gordonsville, Culpepper, Manassas, Alexandria, Washington, Baltimore, Philadelphia, and New York.
First class . . . . - . . . $36.15

ROUTE 718.—NEW YORK TO RICHMOND, CINCINNATI, and return via rail to Philadelphia, Baltimore, steamer down Chesapeake Bay to Fortress Monroe, Norfolk, changing to steamer on James River to City Point, RICHMOND, rail to Orange, Gordonsville, Staunton, Goshen (for Natural Bridge), White Sulphur Springs, Kanawha, Huntington, steamer down Ohio River to CINCINNATI, rail to Chillicothe, Parkersburg, Cumberland, Harper's Ferry, Washington City, Baltimore, Philadelphia, and New York, or vice versa.
First class $40.70

ROUTE 719.—NEW YORK TO CINCINNATI, RICHMOND, and return, via rail to Philadelphia, Harrisburg, Altoona, Pittsburg, Steubenville, Columbus, CINCINNATI, returning by steamer on Ohio River to Huntington, rail through West Virginia to Kanawha, White Sulphur Springs, Goshen (for Natural Bridge), Staunton, Charlotteville, Gordonsville, RICHMOND, steamer down James River to Norfolk, changing to steamer on Chesapeake Bay to Fortress Monroe, Baltimore, rail to Philadelphia, and New York, or vice versa.
First class $40.15

ROUTE 720.—NEW YORK TO RICHMOND, CINCINNATI, and return, via rail to Philadelphia, Baltimore, Washington, steamer on Potomac to Quantico, rail to Fredericksburg, RICHMOND, Gordonsville, Charlotteville, Staunton, Goshen (for Natural Bridge), White Sulphur Springs, Kanawha, Huntington, steamer down Ohio River to CINCINNATI, rail to Chillicothe, Parkersburg, Grafton, Cumberland, Harper's Ferry, Washington, Baltimore, Philadelphia, and New York, or vice versa.
First class $40.40

ROUTE 721.—NEW YORK TO CINCINNATI, RICHMOND, and return, via rail to Philadelphia, Harrisburg, Altoona, Pittsburg, Columbus, CINCINNATI, steamer on Ohio to Huntington, through West Virginia to Kanawha, White

Sulphur Springs, Goshen (for Natural Bridge), Staunton, Charlotteville, Gordonsville, RICHMOND, Fredericksburg, Quantico, steamer on Potomac to Washington City, rail to Baltimore, Philadelphia, and New York, or *vice versa*.
First class $39.85

ROUTE 722.—NEW YORK TO CINCINNATI and return, *via* Philadelphia, Harrisburg, Altoona, Pittsburg, Steubenville, Newark, Columbus, Xenia, CINCINNATI, and back by steamer on Ohio River, to Huntington, rail to Kanawha, White Sulphur Springs, Goshen (for Natural Bridge), Staunton, Harrisonburg, Winchester, Harper's Ferry, Washington City, Baltimore, Philadelphia, and New York.
First class $35.65

ROUTE 723.—NEW YORK TO CINCINNATI and return, same as above to Staunton, then to Charlottesville, Gordonsville, Richmond, Westpoint, steamer up Chesapeake Bay, to Baltimore, rail to Washington, and back to Baltimore, Philadelphia, and New York.
First class $40.00

ROUTE 724.—NEW YORK TO RICHMOND, CINCINNATI and return, *via* Old Dominion Steamship Co. to Fortress Monroe, Norfolk, RICHMOND, rail Gordonsville, Staunton, Goshen (for Natural Bridge), White Sulphur Springs, Huntington, steamer down the Ohio to CINCINNATI, rail to Parkersburg, Cumberland, Harper's Ferry, Washington City, Baltimore, Philadelphia, and New York, or *vice versa*.
First class $44.10

ROUTE 725.—NEW YORK TO CINCINNATI, RICHMOND and return, *via* rail to Philadelphia, Harrrisburg, Altoona, Pittsburg, Columbus, CINCINNATI, steamer up the Ohio to Huntington, rail to White Sulphur Springs, Goshen, Staunton, Gordonsville, RICHMOND, and Old Dominion Steamer direct to New York.
First class $42.90

ROUTE 726.—NEW YORK TO LOUISVILLE and return, *via* Philadelphia, Baltimore, Washington City, Alexandria, Culpepper, Gordonsville, Staunton, Goshen (for Natural Bridge), White Sulphur Springs, Huntington, steamer on Ohio River, to Cincinnati, and rail by Ohio and Mississippi Railway, to North Vernon, Jeffersonville, LOUISVILLE, and back by Short Line to Cincinnati, Chillicothe, Parkersburg, Grafton, Cumberland, Harper's Ferry, Washington City, Baltimore, Philadelphia, and New York, or *vice versa*.
First class $41.60

ROUTE 727.—NEW YORK TO LOUISVILLE and return, *via* Philadelphia, Baltimore, Washington City, Harper's Ferry, Cumberland, Grafton, Parkersburg, Chillicothe, Cincinnati, Covington, LOUISVILLE, and back by Jeffersonville, Cincinnati, steamer on Ohio River to Huntington, rail to Kanawha, White Sulphur Springs, Covington, Goshen (for Natural Bridge), Staunton, Harrisonburg, Strasburg, Winchester, Harper's Ferry, Washington, Baltimore, Philadelphia, and New York, or *vice versa*.
First class $41.10

ROUTE 728.—NEW YORK TO LOUISVILLE and return, *via* Philadelphia, Baltimore, steamer down Chesapeake Bay to Fortress Monroe, West Point, rail to Richmond, Gordonsville, Charlottesville, Staunton, Goshen, Covington, White Sulphur Springs, Kanawha, Huntington, steamer on Ohio River to Cincinnati, rail to North Vernon, Jeffersonville, LOUISVILLE, and back to Covington, Cincinnati, Chillicothe, Parkersburg, Grafton, Cumberland, Harper's Ferry, Washington City, Baltimore, Philadelphia, and New York, or *vice versa*.
First class $42.25

ROUTE 729.—NEW YORK TO LOUISVILLE and return, *via* Philadelphia, Harrisburg, Pittsburgh, Steubenville, Newark, Columbus, Xenia, Cincinnati, North Vernon, Jeffersonville, LOUISVILLE, and back to Covington, Chillicothe,

Parkersburg, Grafton, Cumberland, Harper's Ferry, Washington City, Baltimore, Philadelphia, and New York.
.　First class　.　.　.　.　.　.　.　.　.　$38.45

ROUTE 730.—NEW YORK TO LOUISVILLE and return, same as above to
Cincinnati, thence rail to Covington, LOUISVILLE, and back to Jeffersonville,
North Vernon, Cincinnati, steamer on Ohio River to Huntington, rail to Kan-
awha, White Sulphur Springs, Goshen, Staunton, Charlottesville, Gordonsville,
Alexandria, Washington City, Baltimore, Philadelphia, and New York.
First class　.　.　.　.　.　.　.　.　$41.05

ROUTE 731.—NEW YORK TO LOUISVILLE and return, via same as above
to Louisville and back to Jeffersonville, North Vernon, Cincinnati, steamer on
Ohio River, to Huntington, rail to Kanawha, White Sulphur Springs, Goshen,
Staunton, Harrisonburg, Winchester, Harper's Ferry, Washington City, Balti-
more, Philadelphia, and New York.
First class　.　.　.　.　.　.　$40.60

ROUTE 732.—NEW YORK TO LOUISVILLE and return, via same as above
to Cincinnati, thence North Vernon, Jeffersonville, LOUISVILLE, returning to
Covington, Cincinnati, steamer on Ohio River to Huntington, rail to Kanawha,
White Sulphur Springs, Goshen (for Natural Bridge), Staunton, Charlottesville,
Gordonsville, Richmond, West Point, steamer on Chesapeake Bay to Fortress
Monroe, Baltimore, Philadelphia, and New York.
First class　.　.　.　.　.　$41.70

ROUTE 733.—NEW YORK TO RICHMOND, LOUISVILLE, and return,
via rail to Philadelphia, Baltimore, Washington City, steamer on Potomac, to
Quantico, rail to Fredericksburg, RICHMOND, Gordonsville, Charlottesville,
Staunton, White Sulphur Springs, Kanawha, Huntington, steamer down the
Ohio, to Cincinnati, rail to Covington, LOUISVILLE, Jeffersonville, Cincinnati,
Chillicothe, Parkersburg, Grafton, Cumberland,. Harper's Ferry, Washington,
Baltimore, Philadelphia, and New York, or vice versa.
First class　.　.　.　.　.　.　.　$45.30

ROUTE 734.—NEW YORK TO LOUISVILLE, RICHMOND, and return,
via rail to Philadelphia, Harrisburg, Pittsburg, Steubenville, Columbus, Cincinnati, Covington, LOUISVILLE. Jeffersonville, Cincinnati, steamer on Ohio, to
Huntington, rail through West Virginia, to Kanawha, White Sulphur Springs,
Goshen, Gordonsville, RICHMOND, Fredericksburg, Quantico, steamer on Potomac, to Washington City, rail to Baltimore, Philadelphia, and New York.
First class　.　.　.　.　.　.　.　$44.75

ROUTE 735.—NEW YORK TO RICHMOND, LOUISVILLE, and return,
via rail to Philadelphia, Baltimore, steamer down Chesapeake Bay to Fortress
Monroe, Norfolk, changing to James River steamer to City Point, Richmond,
rail to Orange, Gordonsville, Staunton, Goshen (for Natural Bridge), White
Sulphur Springs, Kanawha, Huntington, steamer on Ohio River to Cincinnati,
rail to Covington, LOUISVILLE, Jeffersonville, Cincinnati, Chillicothe, Parkersburg, Grafton, Cumberland, Harper's Ferry, Washington City, Baltimore,
Philadelphia and New York, or vice versa.
First class　.　.　.　.　.　.　$45.60

ROUTE 736.—NEW YORK TO LOUISVILLE, RICHMOND, and return,
via rail to Philadelphia, Harrisburg, Altoona, Pittsburgh, Steubenville, Newark, Columbia, Cincinnati, Mount Vernon, Jeffersonville, LOUISVILLE, Covington, Cincinnati, steamer up the Ohio River to Huntington, rail through West
Virginia to Kanawha, White Sulphur Springs, Goshen (for Natural Bridge),
Staunton, Charlottesville, Gordonsville, RICHMOND, steamer down James River
to Norfolk, changing to Chesapeake Bay steamer to Fortress Monroe, Baltimore,
rail to Philadelphia and New York.
First class　.　.　.　.　.　.　.　$45.05

ROUTE 737.—NEW YORK TO ST. LOUIS and return, via Philadelphia

Wilmington, Baltimore, Washington City, Harper's Ferry, Cumberland, Grafton, Parkersburg, Cincinnati, Vincennes, St. Louis, and back to Louisville, Covington, Cincinnati, Parkersburg, Grafton, Cumberland, Washington, Baltimore, Philadelphia and New York, or *vice versa.*
First class $50.60

ROUTE 738.—NEW YORK TO ST. LOUIS and return, same as above to St. Louis, thence back to Cincinnati, up the Ohio river by steamer to Huntington, rail to Kanawha, White Sulphur Springs, Covington, Goshen (for Natural Bridge), Staunton, Charlottesville, Gordonsville, Manassas, Alexandria, Washington City, Baltimore, Philadelphia, and back to New York, or *vice versa.*
First class . . . , ... $53.20

ROUTE 739.—NEW YORK TO ST. LOUIS and return, same as above to St. Louis, thence back to Jeffersonville, Louisville, North Vernon, Cincinnati, Parkersburg, Grafton, Cumberland, Harper's Ferry, Washington City, Baltimore, Philadelphia and New York, or *vice versa.*
First class $51.10

ROUTE 740.—NEW YORK TO ST. LOUIS and return, *via* Philadelphia, Baltimore, Washington, Harper's Ferry, Cumberland, Grafton, Parkersburg, Cincinnati, Covington, Louisville, Jeffersonville, St. Louis, returning to Vincennes, Cincinnati, steamer on Ohio River, to Huntington, rail to Kanawha, White Sulphur Springs, West Virginia, Goshen, Staunton, Harrisonburg, Strasburg, Winchester, Harper's Ferry, Washington, Baltimore, Philadelphia and New York, or *vice versa.*
First class $55.75

ROUTE 741.—NEW YORK TO RICHMOND, ST. LOUIS, and return, *via* Philadelphia, Baltimore, steamer down Chesapeake Bay to Ft. Monroe, West Point, rail to Richmond, Gordonsville, Charlottesville, Staunton, Goshen (for Natural Bridge), White Sulphur Springs, Kanawha, Huntington, steamer on Ohio River to Cincinnati, rail to St. Louis, and back to Cincinnati, thence Parkersburg, Grafton, Washington City, Baltimore and Philadelphia or *vice versa.*
First class $51.95

ROUTE 742.—NEW YORK TO ST. LOUIS and return, *via* Philadelphia, Harrisburg, Altoona, Pittsburgh, Steubenville, Newark, Columbus, Cincinnati, Covington, Louisville, Jeffersonville, St. Louis, and back to Vincennes, Cincinnati, Chillicothe, Parkersburg, Grafton, Washington City, Baltimore, Philadelphia and New York.
First class $50.05

ROUTE 743.—NEW YORK TO ST. LOUIS and return, same as above to Cincinnati, thence North Vernon, Jeffersonville, Louisville, St. Louis, returning direct to Cincinnati, steamer on Ohio River to Huntington, thence through West Virginia to Kanawha, White Sulphur Springs, Goshen, Staunton, Charlottesville, Gordonsville, Alexandria, Washington City, Baltimore, Philadelphia and New York.
First class $53.15

ROUTE 744.—NEW YORK TO ST. LOUIS and return, same as above to Cincinnati, thence to Vincennes, St. Louis, returning to Cincinnati, and up the Ohio River to Huntington, by rail through West Virginia to Kanawha, White Sulphur Springs, Goshen, Staunton, Harrisonburg, Strasburg, Winchester, Harper's Ferry, Washington City, Baltimore, Philadelphia and New York.
First class $57 25

ROUTE 745.—NEW YORK TO RICHMOND, ST. LOUIS, and return, *via* rail to Philadelphia, Baltimore, steamer down Chesapeake Bay to Ft. Monroe, Norfolk, changing to steamer on James River to City Point and RICHMOND, rail to Gordonsville, Staunton, Goshen (for Natural Bridge), White Sulphur Springs, Kanawha, Huntington, steamer down Ohio River to Cincinnati, rail to Covington, Louisville, Jeffersonville, Vincennes, St. Louis, returning to Cincinnati,

Chillicothe, Parkersburg, Grafton, Cumberland, Harper's Ferry, Washington City, Baltimore, Philadelphia and New York, or *vice versa.*
First class $57.20

ROUTE 746.—NEW YORK TO ST. LOUIS, RICHMOND, and return, *via* rail to Philadelphia, Harrisburg, Altoona, Pittsburgh, Steubenville, Newark, Columbus, Cincinnati, Vincennes, St. Louis, returning to Vincennes, Mitchell, Jeffersonville, Louisville, Covington, steamer on Ohio River to Huntington; rail through West Virginia to Kanawha, White Sulphur Springs, Goshen (for Natural Bridge), Staunton, Gordonsville, RICHMOND, steamer down James River to City Point and Norfolk, changing into Bay Line steamers for Fortress Monroe, Baltimore, and sail to Philadelphia and New York.
First class $57.65

ROUTE 747.—NEW YORK TO RICHMOND, ST. LOUIS, and return, *via* rail to Philadelphia, Baltimore, Washington City, steamer on Potcmac to Quantico, rail to Fredericksburg, RICHMOND, Charlotteville, Staunton, Goshen, White Sulphur Springs, Huntington, steamer down the Ohio to Cincinnati, rail to Covington, Louisville, Jeffersonville, Vincennes, ST. LOUIS, Cincinnati, Chillicothe, Parkersburg, Grafton, Cumberland, Harper's Ferry, Washington, Baltimore, Philadelphia, and New York, or *vice versa.*
First class $56.90

ROUTE 748.—NEW YORK TO ST. LOUIS, RICHMOND, and return, *via* rail to Philadelphia, Harrisburg, Pittsburgh, Steubenville, Columbus, Cincinnati, Covington, Louisville, Jeffersonville, Vincennes, ST. LOUIS, returning to Cincinnati, and by steamer up the Ohio to Huntington, rail through West Virginia to Kanawha, White Sulphur Springs, Goshen (for Natural Bridge), Staunton, Charlotteville, RICHMOND, steamer to Norfolk, Fortress Monroe, Baltimore, rail to Philadelphia and New York.
First class $56.05

ROUTE 749.—NEW YORK TO ST. LOUIS and return, *via* Philadelphia, Harrisburg, Altoona, Pittsburg, Steubenville, Newark, Columbus, Cincinnati, Covington, Louisville, Jeffersonville, Vincennes, ST. LOUIS, returning to Cincinnati, Chillicothe, Parkersburg, Grafton, Cumberland, Harper's Ferry, Winchester, Strasburg, Staunton, Charlotteville, Gordonsville, Richmond. West Point, steamer on Chesapeake Bay to Fortress Monroe, Baltimore, rail to Washington, and back to Baltimore, Philadelphia, and New York.
First class $55.35

ROUTE 750.—NEW YORK TO KANSAS CITY and return, *via* Philadelphia, Baltimore, Washington City, Alexandria, Manassas, Gordonsville, Charlotteville, Staunton, Goshen, Covington, White Sulphur Springs, Kanawha, Huntington, steamer down Ohio River to Cincinnati, rail to Covington, Louisville, Jeffersonville, St. Louis, Mexico, KANSAS CITY, and back to St. Louis, Cincinnati, Chillicothe, Parkersburg, Grafton, Cumberland, Harper's Ferry, Washington, Baltimore, Philadelphia, and New York, or *vice versa.*
First class $67.20

ROUTE 751.—NEW YORK TO KANSAS CITY and return, *via* Philadelphia, Baltimore, Harper's Ferry, Cumberland, Grafton, Parkersburg, Chillicothe, Cincinnati, Vincennes, St. Louis, Mexico, KANSAS CITY, and back to St. Louis, Jeffersonville, Louisville, Covington, Cincinnati, steamer up Ohio River to Huntington, rail through West Virginia to Kanawha, White Sulphur Springs, Goshen, Staunton, Harrisonburg, Strasburg, Winchester, Harper's Ferry, Washington City, Baltimore, Philadelphia, and New York, or *vice versa.*
First class $68.90

ROUTE 752.—NEW YORK TO KANSAS CITY and return, *via* Philadelphia, Harrisburg, Altoona, Pittsburg, Steubenville, Newark, Columbus, Cincinnati, Covington, Louisville, Jeffersonville, Vincennes, St. Louis, Mexico, KANSAS CITY, returning to St. Louis, Cincinnati, Chillicothe, Parkersburg,

Grafton, Cumberland, Harper's Ferry, Washington City, Baltimore, Philadelphia, and New York.

First class $64.05

ROUTE 753.—NEW YORK TO KANSAS CITY and return, same as above to KANSAS CITY, returning to St. Louis, Cincinnati, steamer on Ohio River to Huntington, rail through West Virginia to Kanawha, White Sulphur Sp.ings, Goshen, Staunton, Gordonsville, Alexandria, Washington City, Baltimore, Philadelphia, and New York.

First class $66.65

ROUTE 754.—NEW YORK TO KANSAS CITY and return, same as above to Cincinnati, thence North Vernon, Jeffersonville, Louisville, Vincennes, St. Louis, Mexico, KANSAS CITY, returning to Cincinnati by same route, thence steamer on Ohio River to Huntington, thence rail to West Virginia to White Sulphur Springs, Goshen, Staunton, Harrisonburg, Strasburg, Winchester, Harper's Ferry, Washington City, Baltimore, Philadelphia, and New York.

First class $66.65

TOURS COMBINING

The Pennsylvania Oil Regions, Niagara Falls, Washington City, River St. Lawrence, Montreal, &c.

ROUTE 755.—NEW YORK TO OIL REGIONS and return, via rail to Philadelphia, Baltimore, Washington City, Harper's Ferry, Cumberland, Alleghany Mountains, Pittsburg, Kittanning, Franklin, Oil City, Corry, Brockton, Buffalo, Rochester, Syracuse, Albany, and (rail or boat) down the Hudson to New York, or vice versa.

First class $27.00

ROUTE 756.—NEW YORK TO OIL REGIONS and return, via Erie Railway to Elmira, Buffalo, Brockton, Corry, Oil City, Franklin, Alleghany River, Kittanning, Pittsburg, Monongahela River, Alleghany Mountains, Cumberland, Harper's Ferry, Washington City, Baltimore, Philadelphia, and New York, or vice versa.

First class . . . . . : $27.00

ROUTE 757.—NEW YORK TO SARATOGA, NIAGARA FALLS, OIL REGIONS, and return, via Hudson River (rail or boat) to Troy, rail to SARATOGA, Schenectady, Syracuse, Rochester, NIAGARA FALLS, Buffalo, Brocton, Corry, Oil City, Franklin, Alleghany River, Pittsburg, Monongahela River, Cumberland, Harper's Ferry, Washington City, Baltimore, Philadelphia, and New York, or vice versa.

First class $29.25

ROUTE 758.—NEW YORK TO NIAGARA FALLS, OIL REGIONS, and return, via Erie Railway to Elmira (for Watkins Glen), Hornellsville, NIAGARA FALLS, Buffalo, Brocton. Marysville (Lake Chatauqua), Corry, Oil City, Franklin, Alleghany River, Kittanning, Pittsburg, Monongahela River, Alleghany Mountains, Cumberland, Harper's Ferry, Washington City, Baltimore, Philadelphia, and New York, or vice versa.

First class $27.25

ROUTE 759.—NEW YORK TO OIL REGIONS, NIAGARA FALLS, and return, via Philadelphia, Baltimore, Washington City, Harper's Ferry, Cumberland, Alleghany Mountains, Monongahela River, Pittsburg, Alleghan

River, Kittanning, Franklin, Oil City, Corry, Marysville (Chatauqua Lake), Brocton, Buffalo, Niagara Falls, Rochester, Syracuse, Albany, and down the Hudson (by rail or boat) to New York, or *vice versa*.

First class $27.55

ROUTE 760.—NEW YORK TO CANADA, NIAGARA FALLS, OIL REGIONS, and return, *via* Hudson River (rail or boat) to Albany, Rome, Cape Vincent, steamer across Lake Ontario to Kingston, rail to Toronto, Hamilton, Suspension Bridge, Niagara Falls, Buffalo, Brocton, Marysville (Chatauqua Lake), Corry, Oil City, Franklin, Alleghany River, Kittanning, Pittsburg, Monongahela River, Alleghany Mountains, Cumberland, Harper's Ferry, Washington City, Baltimore, and New York, or *vice versa*.

First class $36.50

ROUTE 761.—NEW YORK TO RICHMOND, OIL REGIONS, NIAGARA FALLS, and return, *via* rail to Philadelphia, Baltimore, Washington, steamer down Potomac to RICHMOND, rail to Gordonsville, Staunton, Harrisonburg, Strasburg, Winchester, Cumberland, Pittsburg, Oil City, Corry, Brocton, Buffalo, NIAGARA FALLS, Syracuse, Albany, and down the Hudson (by boat or rail) to New York, or *vice versa*.

First class $39.35

ROUTE 762.—NEW YORK TO RICHMOND, OIL REGIONS, NIAGARA FALLS, and return, *via* rail to Philadelphia, Baltimore, steamer, down Chesapeake Bay to West Point, rail to RICHMOND, Gordonsville, Alexandria, Washington City, Harper's Ferry, Cumberland, Pittsburg, Oil City, Corry, Brocton, Buffalo, Niagara Falls, thence to New York by the Erie or New York Central Railroads, or *vice versa*.

First class $36.25

ROUTE 763.—NEW YORK TO RICHMOND, OIL REGIONS, NIAGARA FALLS, and return, *via* same route as above to Richmond, thence rail to Fredericksburg, Quantico, and steamer up the Potomac to Washington, thence rail to Harper's Ferry, Cumberland, Pittsburg, Oil City, Corry, Brocton, Buffalo, NIAGARA FALLS, thence to New York by the New York Central or Erie Railway, or *vice versa*.

First class $35.70

ROUTE 764.—NEW YORK TO OIL REGIONS, NIAGARA FALLS, MONTREAL, and return, *via* rail to Philadelphia, Baltimore, Washington City, Cumberland, Pittsburg, Alleghany River, Oil City, Corry, Brocton, Buffalo, NIAGARA FALLS, Toronto, steamer on Lake Ontario to 1000 Islands, Rapids of St. Lawrence, MONTREAL, Lake Champlain, White Hall, Saratoga, Albany, and down Hudson (by rail or boat) to New York.

First class $44.70

ROUTE 765.—NEW YORK TO OIL REGIONS, NIAGARA FALLS, MONTREAL, BOSTON, and return, *via* same as above to Montreal, thence rail to Portland, Boston, and Fall River, steamer to New York.

First class $45.35

ROUTE 766.—NEW YORK TO OIL REGIONS, NIAGARA FALLS, MONTREAL, and return, *via* rail to Philadelphia, Baltimore, Washington, Cumberland, Pittsburg, Oil City, Corry, Brocton, Buffalo, NIAGARA FALLS, Toronto, steamer to Kingston, 1000 Islands, Rapids of St. Lawrence, MONTREAL, Rouse's Point, Lake Champlain, Lake George, Saratoga, Albany, and down the Hudson by rail or boat.

First class $47.90

ROUTE 767.—NEW YORK TO OIL REGIONS, NIAGARA FALLS, MONTREAL, BOSTON, and return, *via* rail to Philadelphia, Baltimore, Washington City, Cumberland, Pittsburg, Oil City, Corry, Brocton, Buffalo, NIAGARA FALLS, Toronto, steamer to Kingston, 1000 Islands, Rapids of St. Lawrence, MONTREAL, St. Johns, Newport (Lake Memphremagog), White River Junction, Concord, Nashua, BOSTON, and Sound steamers to New York.

First class $47.70

ROUTE 768.—NEW YORK TO OIL REGIONS, NIAGARA FALLS, MON-
TREAL, QUEBEC, BOSTON, and return, *via* rail to Philadelphia, Baltimore,
Washington, Cumberland, Pittsburg, Oil City, Corry, Brocton, Buffalo, NIAG-
ARA FALLS, Toronto, steamer on Lake Ontario to 1000 Islands, Rapids of St.
Lawrence, MONTREAL, QUEBEC, rail to Portland, BOSTON, and Fall River,
steamer to New York.
First class $48.35

ROUTE 769.—NEW YORK TO OIL REGIONS, NIAGARA FALLS, MON-
TREAL, QUEBEC, BOSTON, and return, *via* same route as above to NIAGARA
FALLS, Toronto, steamer on Lake Ontario to Kingston, 1000 Islands, Rapids of
St. Lawrence, MONTREAL, QUEBEC, Sherbrooke, Newport (Lake Memphrema-
gog), White River Junction, Concord, Nashua, Boston, and Fall River steamer
to New York.
First class $49.70

ROUTE 770.—NEW YORK TO CAPE VINCENT, CANADA, NIAGARA
FALLS, OIL REGIONS, and return, *via* (rail or boat) up the Hudson to Al-
bany, rail to Rome, Cape Vincent, steamer across Lake Ontario to Kingston,
rail to Toronto, NIAGARA FALLS, Buffalo, Brocton, Corry, Oil City, Pittsburg,
Cumberland, Harper's Ferry, Washington City, Baltimore, Philadelphia, New
York, or *vice versa*.
First class $36.60

TOURS COMBINING

West Virginia, Lake Erie, Canada and Niagara Falls.

ROUTE 771.—NEW YORK TO DETROIT and return, *via* rail to Philadel-
phia, Baltimore, Washington City, Cumberland, Wheeling, Newark, Mansfield,
Sandusky, steamer Jay Cooke to Put in Bay, DETROIT, rail to Hamilton, Nia-
gara Falls, Rochester, Albany, and down the Hudson by rail or boat to New
York, or *vice versa*.
First class , ... $35.95

ROUTE 772.—NEW YORK TO DETROIT and return, *via* rail to Philadelphia, Baltimore, Washington City, Cumberland, Wheeling, Newark, Mansfield,
Sandusky, steamer Jay Cooke to Put in Bay, DETROIT, rail to Niagara Falls,
and by Erie Railway to New York, or *vice versa*.
First class $35.05

ROUTE 773.—NEW YORK TO DETROIT and return, *via* rail to Philadel-
phia, Baltimore, Washington City, Cumberland, Wheeling, Newark, Mansfield,
Sandusky, steamer Jay Coeke to Put in Bay, DETROIT, steamer to Cleveland,
steamer to Buffalo, rail to Niagara Falls, Rochester, Albany, and down the
Hudson by rail or boat to New York, or *vice versa*.
First class $36.60

COOK'S CIRCULAR TOURS TO THE WEST,

COMBINING

Niagara Falls, Chicago, St. Louis, Louisville, Cincinnati, and West Virginia.

ROUTE 801.—NEW YORK TO CHICAGO, ST. LOUIS, CINCINNATI,
and return, *via* Hudson River to Albany (rail or boat), Syracuse, Rochester, Niagara, Falls, Suspension Bridge, through Canada to Hamilton, London,
Detroit, Kalamazoo, CHICAGO, Springfield, ST. LOUIS, Vincennes, Jeffersonville, Louisville, CINCINNATI, Chillicothe, Parkersburg, Grafton, Cumberland,

Harper's Ferry, Washington City, Baltimore, Philadelphia, and New York, or *vice versa.*
First class $53.70

ROUTE 802.—NEW YORK TO CHICAGO, ST. LOUIS, CINCINNATI, and return, *via* Erie Railway to Elmira, Buffalo, Niagara Falls, Suspension Bridge, and same as above to New York, or *vice versa.*
First class $53.70

ROUTE 803.—NEW YORK TO CHICAGO, ST. LOUIS, CINCINNATI, and return, *via* Hudson River to Albany (rail or boat), rail to Syracuse, Rochester, Niagara Falls, Suspension Bridge, through Canada to Hamilton, London, Detroit, Kalamazoo, CHICAGO, Springfield, ST. LOUIS, Vincennes, Jeffersonville, Louisville, Covington, CINCINNATI, steamer on Ohio River to Huntington, rail through West Virginia to Kanawha, White Sulphur Springs, Goshen, Staunton, Charlotteville, Gordonsville, Manassas, Alexandria, Washington City, Baltimore, Philadelphia, and New York, or *vice versa.*
First class $56.30

ROUTE 804.—NEW YORK TO CHICAGO, ST. LOUIS, CINCINNATI, and return, *via* Erie Railway to Elmira, Buffalo, Niagara Falls, and same as above back to New York, or *vice versa.*
First class $56.30

ROUTE 805.—NEW YORK TO CHICAGO, ST. LOUIS, CINCINNATI, and return, *via* Hudson River (rail or boat), to Albany, rail to Syracuse, Rochester, Niagara Falls, Suspension Bridge, through Canada to Hamilton, London, Detroit, Kalamazoo, CHICAGO, Springfield, ST. LOUIS, Vincennes, Jeffersonville, Louisville, Covington, CINCINNATI, steamer up Ohio River to Huntington, rail through West Virginia to Kanawha, White Sulphur Springs, Goshen (for Natural Bridge), Staunton, up the Valley of Virginia to Harrisonburg, Strasburg, Winchester, Harper's Ferry, Washington City, Baltimore, Philadelphia, and New York, or *vice versa.*
First class $55.80

ROUTE 806.—NEW YORK TO CHICAGO, ST. LOUIS, CINCINNATI, and return, *via* Erie Railway, to Elmira, Buffalo, Niagara Falls, and same as above, back to New York, or *vice versa.*
First class $55.80

ROUTE 807.—NEW YORK TO CHICAGO, ST. LOUIS, CINCINNATI, RICHMOND, and return, *via* Hudson River (rail or boat), to Albany, rail to Syracuse, Rochester, Niagara Falls, Suspension Bridge, through Canada, to Hamilton, London, Detroit, Kalamazoo, CHICAGO, Springfield, ST. LOUIS, Vincennes, Cincinnati, Chillicothe, Parkersburg, Grafton, Cumberland, Harper's Ferry, Winchester, Strasburg, Staunton, Gordonsville, RICHMOND, West Point, steamer on Chesapeake Bay to Fortress Monroe, Baltimore, rail to Philadelphia, and back to New York, or *vice versa.*
First class $61.65

ROUTE 808.—NEW YORK TO CHICAGO, ST. LOUIS, RICHMOND, and return, *via* Erie Railway, to Elmira, Niagara Falls, and same as above, back to New York, or *vice versa.*
First class $61.65

ROUTE 809.—NEW YORK TO CHICAGO, ST. LOUIS, RICHMOND, and return, *via* Erie Railway, to Elmira, Buffalo, Niagara Falls, Suspension Bridge, London, Detroit, CHICAGO, Springfield, ST. LOUIS, Vincennes, Jeffersonville, Louisville, Jeffersonville, Cincinnati, steamer on Ohio River, to Huntington, rail through West Virginia, to Kanawha, White Sulphur Springs, Goshen, stage to Lexington, Natural Bridge, Bonsacks, Lynchburg, Burkeville, RICHMOND, Gordonsville, Culpepper, Alexandria, Washington City, Baltimore, Philadelphia, or *vice versa.*
First class $72.40

ROUTE 810.—NEW YORK TO CHICAGO, ST. LOUIS, RICHMOND, and return; *via* Hudson River (rail or boat), to Albany, rail to Syracuse, Rochester, Niagara Falls, Suspension Bridge, and same as above, back to New York, or *vice versa.*
First class $72.40

ROUTE 811.—NEW YORK TO CHICAGO, ST. LOUIS, RICHMOND, and return, *via* Hudson River (rail or boat), to Albany, rail to Syracuse, Rochester, Niagara Falls, Suspension Bridge, across Canada, to Hamilton, London, Detroit, Kalamazoo, CHICAGO, Springfield, ST. LOUIS, Vincennes, Jeffersonville, Louisville, Covington, Cincinnati, steamer on Ohio River, to Huntington, rail through West Virginia, to Kanawha, White Sulphur Springs, Goshen, Staunton, Charlottesville, RICHMOND, Gordonsville, Culpepper, Manassas, Alexandria, Washington City, Baltimore, Philadelphia, and New York, or *vice versa.*
First class $60.45

ROUTE 812.—NEW YORK TO CHICAGO, ST. LOUIS, RICHMOND, and return, *via* Erie Railway, to Elmira, Buffalo, Niagara Falls, and same as above, back to New York, or *vice versa.*
First class $60.45

ROUTE 813.—NEW YORK TO CHICAGO, ST. LOUIS, RICHMOND, and return, *via* Hudson River (rail or boat), to Albany, rail to Syracuse, Rochester, Niagara Falls, Hamilton, Detroit, CHICAGO, Springfield, ST. LOUIS, Vincennes, Cincinnati, steamer on Ohio, to Huntington, rail to White Sulphur Springs, Staunton, RICHMOND, Fredericksburg, Quantico, steamer on Potomac, to Washington City, rail to Baltimore, Washington, Philadelphia, and New York, or *vice versa.*
First class $58.10

ROUTE 814.—NEW YORK TO CHICAGO, ST. LOUIS, RICHMOND, and return, *via* Erie Railway, to Elmira, Buffalo, Niagara Falls, Suspension Bridge, and same as above, back to New York, or *vice versa.*
First class $58.10

ROUTE 815.—NEW YORK TO CHICAGO, ST. LOUIS, RICHMOND, and return, *via* Hudson River to Albany (rail or boat), Syracuse, Rochester, Niagara Falls, Suspension Bridge, Hamilton, London, Detroit, Kalamazoo, CHICAGO, Springfield, ST. LOUIS, Vincennes, Jeffersonville, Louisville, Covington, Cincinnati, steamer on Ohio River, to Huntington, rail through West Virginia, to Kanawha, White Sulphur Springs, Goshen (for Natural Bridge), Staunton, Charlottesville, RICHMOND, steamer down James River, to Norfolk, changing into steamer of the Bay Line, up Chesapeake Bay to Fortress Monroe, Baltimore, rail to Philadelphia, and New York, or *vice versa.*
First class $60.30

ROUTE 816.—NEW YORK TO CHICAGO, ST. LOUIS, RICHMOND, and return, *via* Erie Railway, to Elmira, Buffalo, Niagara Falls, Suspension Bridge, and same as above, back to New York, or *vice versa.*
First class $60.30

ROUTE 817.—NEW YORK TO CHICAGO, WEST VIRGINIA, and return, *via* Hudson River (rail or boat), to Albany, rail to Syracuse, Rochester, Niagara Falls, Suspension Bridge, Hamilton, London, Detroit, Kalamazoo, CHICAGO, Springfield, ST. LOUIS, Vincennes, Jeffersonville, Louisville, Covington, Cincinnati, steamer up the Ohio River, to Huntington, rail through West Virginia, to Kanawha, White Sulphur Springs, Goshen, stage to Lexington, Natural Bridge, Bonsacks, rail to Lynchburg, Petersburg, Norfolk, and steamer up Chesapeake Bay to Fortress Monroe, Baltimore, rail to Philadelphia, and New York, or *vice versa.*
First class $72.90

28 COOK'S AMERICAN TOURS.

Route 818.—NEW YORK, CHICAGO, ST. LOUIS, WEST VIRGINIA, and return, *via* Erie Railway, to Elmira, Buffalo, Niagara Falls, Suspension Bridge, and same as above, back to New York, or *vice versa*.
First class $72.90

Tours to Chicago, St. Louis, etc., omitting Niagara Falls.

Route 819.—NEW YORK TO CHICAGO, ST. LOUIS, and return, *via* Philadelphia, Harrisburg, Altoona, Pittsburg, Fort Wayne, Chicago, Bloomington, Springfield, St. Louis, Vincennes, Jeffersonville, Louisville, Covington, Cincinnati, Chillicothe, Parkersburg, Grafton, Cumberland, Harper's Ferry, Washington City, Baltimore, Philadelphia, and New York.
First class $51.05

Route 820.—NEW YORK TO CHICAGO, ST. LOUIS, and return, *via* Hudson River (rail or boat), to Albany, rail to Syracuse, Rochester, Buffalo, Port Colborne, Stratford, Sarnia, Detroit, Kalamazoo, Chicago, Bloomington, Springfield, St. Louis, Vincennes, Jeffersonville, Louisville, Covington, Cincinnati, Chillicothe, Parkersburg, Grafton, Cumberland, Harper's Ferry, Washington City, Baltimore, Philadelphia, and New York, or *vice versa*.
First class $55.80

Route 821.—NEW YORK TO CHICAGO, ST. LOUIS, and return, *via* Erie Railway, to Elmira, Buffalo, and same as above, back to New York, or *vice versa*.
First class $55.80

Route 822.—NEW YORK TO CHICAGO, ST. LOUIS, RICHMOND, and return, *via* Philadelphia, Harrisburg, Altoona, Pittsburgh, Fort Wayne, Chicago, Bloomington, Springfield, St. Louis, Vincennes, Jeffersonville, Louisville, Covington, Cincinnati, steamer on Ohio River, to Huntington, rail through West Virginia, to Kanawha, White Sulphur Springs, Goshen (for Natural Bridge), Staunton, Charlottesville, Richmond, steamer down James River, to Norfolk, changing to steamer on Chesapeake Bay to Fortress Monroe, Baltimore, rail to Baltimore, and Philadelphia, and New York.
First class $57.65

Route 823.—NEW YORK TO CHICAGO, ST. LOUIS, RICHMOND, and return, *via* Hudson River (rail or boat), to Albany, rail to Syracuse, Buffalo (or by Erie Railway to Buffalo), Port Colborne, Stratford, Sarnia, Detroit, Kalamazoo, Chicago, Bloomington, Springfield, St. Louis, Vincennes, Jeffersonville, Louisville, Covington, Cincinnati, and same as above, back to New York, or *vice versa*.
First class $62.40

Route 824.—NEW YORK TO CHICAGO, ST. LOUIS, RICHMOND, and return, *via* Philadelphia, Harrisburgh, Pittsburgh, Fort Wayne, Chicago, Bloomington, Springfield, St. Louis, Vincennes, Jeffersonville, Louisville, Covington, Cincinnati, steamer up the Ohio River, to Huntington, rail through West Virginia, to Kanawha, White Sulphur Springs, Goshen (for Natural Bridge), Staunton, Charlottesville, Gordonsville, Richmond, Fair Oaks, West Point, steamer on York River, and Chesapeake Bay to Fortress Monroe, Baltimore, rail to Philadelphia, and New York.
First class $54.30

Route 825.—NEW YORK TO CHICAGO, ST. LOUIS, RICHMOND, and return, *via* same Route as above, to Richmond, thence by rail to Fredericksburg, Quantico, steamer on Potomac, to Washington City, rail to Baltimore, Philadelphia, and New York.
First class $57.35

Route 826.—NEW YORK TO CHICAGO and return, *via* Philadelphia,

Harrisburg, Pittsburg, Fort Wayne, CHICAGO, Detroit, Niagara Falls, Rochester, Albany, and down Hudson (by rail or boat) to New York.

First class $40.00

ROUTE 827.—NEW YORK TO CHICAGO and return, via Philadelphia,
Pittsburg, Fort Wayne, CHICAGO, Detroit, Niagara Falls, Buffalo, Elmira, and
Erie Railway to New York.

First class $40.00

ROUTE 828.—NEW YORK TO CHICAGO and return, via Philadelphia,
Pittsburg, Fort Wayne, CHICAGO, Detroit, Port Colborne, Buffalo, and thence
to New York, by either the Erie or New York Central Railways.

First class $42.15

ROUTE 829.—NEW YORK TO CHICAGO and return, via Pittsburg, Fort
Wayne, CHICAGO, Detroit, Toronto, Kingston, steamer across Lake Ontario to
Cape Vincent, rail to Rome, Albany, and by rail or boat down the Hudson to
New York.

First class . . . $46.75

Tours to the West, Omaha, Denver, Colorado Springs, Rocky Mountains, &c.

ROUTE 850.—NEW YORK TO KANSAS CITY and return, via Hudson
River to Albany (rail or boat), Syracuse, Rochester, Niagara Falls, Hamilton,
London, Detroit, Kalamazoo, Chicago, Bloomington, Mexico, KANSAS CITY,
and back to Mexico, St. Louis, Vincennes, Cincinnati, Chillicothe, Parkersburg,
Cumberland, Harper's Ferry, Washington City, Baltimore, Philadelphia, and
New York, or vice versa.

First class $63.95

ROUTE 851.—NEW YORK TO KANSAS CITY and return, via Erie Railway to Elmira, Buffalo, Niagara Falls, Suspension Bridge, and same as above
back to New York, or vice versa.

First class $63.95

ROUTE 852.—NEW YORK TO KANSAS CITY and return, via Hudson
River (rail or boat) to Albany, rail to Syracuse, Rochester, Niagara Falls, Sus-
pension Bridge, Hamilton, London, Detroit, Kalamazoo, Chicago, Bloomington,
Mexico, KANSAS CITY, returning same way to Niagara Falls, thence by Erie
Railway to Buffalo, Attica, Hornellsville, Elmira, and New York, or vice versa.

First class $65.25

ROUTE 853.—NEW YORK TO KANSAS CITY and return, via Philadelphia, Harrisburg, Pittsburg, Fort Wayne, Chicago, Bloomington, Mexico,
KANSAS CITY, St. Louis, Vincennes, Cincinnati, Chillicothe, Parkersburg,
Grafton, Cumberland, Harper's Ferry, Washington, Baltimore, Philadelphia,
and New York.

First class $61.30

ROUTE 854.—NEW YORK TO KANSAS CITY and return, via same route
as above to Kansas City, returning to Mexico, Chicago, Detroit, London, Niagara Falls, Rochester, Syracuse, Albany, and down Hudson (by rail or boat) to
New York, or by Erie Railway from Niagara Falls to New York.

First class $62.60

ROUTE 855.—NEW YORK TO KANSAS CITY and return, via Hudson
River (rail or boat) to Albany, rail to Syracuse, Rochester, Niagara Falls, Suspension Bridge, Hamilton, London, Detroit, Kalamazoo, Chicago, Bloomington, Mexico, KANSAS CITY, Mexico, St. Louis, Springfield, Bloomington,
Chicago, Detroit, Niagara Falls, Buffalo, Attica, Elmira, New York, or vice
versa.

First class $67.05

30   COOK'S AMERICAN TOURS.

ROUTE 856.—NEW YORK TO OMAHA, KANSAS CITY, and return, via Hudson River (rail or boat) to Albany, rail to Syracuse, Rochester, Niagara Falls, Suspension Bridge, Hamilton, London, Detroit, Chicago, OMAHA, St. Josephs, Leavenworth, KANSAS CITY, Mexico, St. Louis, Vincennes, Cincinnati, Parkersburg, Grafton, Cumberland, Washington City, Baltimore, Philadelphia, and New York, or vice versa.
First class $74.80

ROUTE 857.—NEW YORK TO OMAHA, KANSAS CITY, and return, via Elmira and Erie Railway to Buffalo, Niagara Falls, and same as above back to New York, or vice versa.
First class $74.80

ROUTE 858.—NEW YORK TO OMAHA, KANSAS CITY, and return, via Philadelphia, Harrisburg, Pittsburg, Fort Wayne, Chicago, OMAHA, St. Josephs, Leavenworth, KANSAS CITY, Mexico, St. Louis, Vincennes, Cincinnati, Chillicothe, Parkersburg, Grafton, Cumberland, Harper's Ferry, Washington City, Baltimore, Philadelphia, and New York.
First class $72.15

ROUTE 859.—NEW YORK TO KANSAS CITY and return, via same route as above to Omaha, thence to St Josephs, Leavenworth, KANSAS CITY, Mexico, Bloomington, Chicago, Detroit, through Canada to Niagara Falls, Rochester, Syracuse, Albany, and down Hudson (rail or boat) to New York, or by Erie Railway from Niagara Falls, via Buffalo and Elmira to New York.
First class $73.40

ROUTE 860.—NEW YORK TO DENVER and return, via rail to Philadelphia, Baltimore, Washington City, Harper's Ferry, Cumberland, Parkersburg, Cincinnati, St. Louis, Kansas City, over the great Buffalo Plains to DENVER, and return the same way.
First class $117.70

ROUTE 861.—NEW YORK TO DENVER and return, via rail to Philadelphia, Harrisburg, Pittsburg, Columbus, Cincinnati, St. Louis, Kansas City, over the great Buffalo Plains to DENVER, returning to Kansas City, St. Louis, Cincinnati, Parkersburg, Washington, Baltimore, Philadelphia, and New York.
First class $117.15

ROUTE 862.—NEW YORK TO DENVER and return, via Philadelphia, Harrisburg, Pittsburg, Fort Wayne, Chicago, Bloomington, Mexico, Kansas City, Lawrence, Topeka, and across the great Buffalo Country, by the Kansas Pacific Railway to DENVER, returning same way to Kansas City, Mexico, St. Louis, Vincennes, Cincinnati, Parkersburg, Cumberland, Washington City, Baltimore, Philadelphia, and New York.
First class $116.30

ROUTE 863.—NEW YORK TO DENVER and return, same as above to Denver, returning to Kansas City, Mexico, St. Louis, Springfield, Bloomington, Chicago, Kalamazoo, Detroit, through Canada to Suspension Bridge, Niagara Falls, Rochester, Syracuse, Albany, and down the Hudson (by rail or boat) to New York (or from Niagara Falls by Erie Railway) to Buffalo, Elmira, and New York.
First class $119.40

ROUTE 864.—NEW YORK TO DENVER and return, via rail to Philadelphia, Baltimore, Washington City, Cumberland, Parkersburg, Cincinnati, Covington, Louisville, Jeffersonville, Vincennes, St. Louis, Mexico, Kansas City, Lawrence, Topeka, and across the Buffalo Country by the Kansas Pacific Railway to DENVER, returning same route to Kansas City, thence to Mexico, Bloomington, Chicago, Kalamazoo, Detroit, through Canada to Niagara Falls, Rochester, Syracuse, Albany, and down the Hudson (by rail or boat) to New York, or vice versa.
First class $120.85

ROUTE 865.—NEW YORK TO DENVER and return, *via* Erie Railway to Elmira, Attica, Buffalo, Niagara Falls, Suspension Bridge, Hamilton, London, Detroit, Kalamazoo, Chicago, Bloomington, Mexico, Kansas City, Lawrence, Topeka, and across the great Buffalo Plains by the Kansas Pacific Railway to DENVER, returning same way to Kansas City, Mexico, St. Louis, Vincennes, Jeffersonville, Louisville, Covington, Cincinnati, Chillicothe, Parkersburg, Cumberland, Harper's Ferry, Washington City, Baltimore, Philadelphia, and New York, or *vice versa*.
First class $120.85

ROUTE 866.—NEW YORK TO DENVER and return, *via* Philadelphia, Harrisburg, Pittsburg, Fort Wayne, Chicago, Bloomington, Mexico, Kansas City, Lawrence, Topeka, and over the great Buffalo Plains to DENVER by the Kansas Pacific Railway, returning same route to Kansas City, Mexico, St. Louis, Vincennes, Jeffersonville, Louisville, Covington, Cincinnati, Chillicothe, Parkersburg, Grafton, Cumberland, Washington City, Baltimore, Washington City, Philadelphia, and New York. .
First class $118.20

ROUTE 867.—NEW YORK TO OMAHA, DENVER, and return, *via* Hudson River (rail or boat) to Albany, rail to Syracuse, Rochester, Niagara Falls, Suspension Bridge, Hamilton, London, Detroit, Kalamazoo, Chicago, OMAHA, St. Josephs, Leavenworth, Kansas City, Topeka, and over the Buffalo Plains to DENVER, returning to Kansas City, Mexico, St. Louis, Vincennes, Jeffersonville, Louisville, Cincinnati, Parkersburg, Cumberland, Washington City, Baltimore, Philadelphia, and New York, or *vice versa*.
First class $131.70

ROUTE 868.—NEW YORK TO DENVER, OMAHA, and return, *via* Philadelphia, Baltimore, Washington City, Harper's Ferry, Cumberland, Parkersburg, Cincinnati, Louisville, Jeffersonville, Vincennes, St. Louis, Mexico, Kansas City, Lawrence, Topeka, across the Buffalo Plains to DENVER, returning same way to Kansas City, Leavenworth, St. Josephs, OMAHA, Cedar Rapids, Chicago, Kalamazoo, Detroit, Niagara Falls, Buffalo, Elmira, New York, or *vice versa*.
First class . . . - $131.70

ROUTE 869.—NEW YORK TO DENVER, COLORADO SPRINGS, THE ROCKY MOUNTAINS, and return, *via* Hudson River (rail or boat) to Albany, rail to Rochester, Niagara Falls, Detroit, Chicago, Bloomington, Mexico, Kansas City, Topeka, across the great Buffalo Plains to Denver and COLORADO SPRINGS, returning same way to Mexico, thence rail to St. Louis, Vincennes, Cincinnati, Parkersburg, Washington City, Baltimore, Philadelphia, and New York, or *vice versa*.
First class $128.95

ROUTE 870.—NEW YORK TO DENVER, COLORADO SPRINGS, ROCKY MOUNTAINS, and return, *via* Philadelphia, Baltimore, Washington City, Parkersburg, Cincinnati, St. Louis, Kansas City, Denver, COLORADO SPRINGS, and back to New York the same way.
First class $127.70

ROUTE 871.—NEW YORK TO DENVER, COLORADO SPRINGS, PUEBLO, ROCKY MOUNTAINS, and return, *via* Hudson River (rail or boat) to Albany, rail to Niagara Falls, Detroit, Chicago, Bloomington, Kansas City, Denver, Colorado Springs, PUEBLO, and back to Kansas City, St. Louis, Vincennes, Cincinnati, Parkersburg, Cumberland, Washington City, Baltimore, Philadelphia, and New York, or *vice versa*.
First class $133.95

ROUTE 872.—NEW YORK TO DENVER, COLORADO SPRINGS, PUEBLO, ROCKY MOUNTAINS, and return, *via* Philadelphia, Baltimore,

32 COOK'S AMERICAN TOURS.

Washington City, Cumberland, Parkersburg, Cincinnati, St. Louis, DENVER, COLORADO SPRINGS, PUEBLO, and back same way to New York.
First class $132.70

Tours to California, Salt Lake, The Yosemite Valley, The Geysers, &c.

ROUTE 873.—NEW YORK TO SALT LAKE, SAN FRANCISCO, and return, via Hudson River (rail or boat) to Albany, rail to Syracuse, Rochester, Niagara Falls, Hamilton, Detroit, Chicago, Omaha, Ogden, SALT LAKE CITY, Sacramento, SAN FRANCISCO, returning to Omaha, St. Josephs, Leavenworth, Kansas City, Mexico, St. Louis, Vincennes, Cincinnati, Parkersburg, Cumberland, Washington City, Baltimore, Philadelphia, and New York, or vice versa.
First class $276.30

ROUTE 874.—NEW YORK TO SALT LAKE, SAN FRANCISCO, and return, via Philadelphia, Baltimore, Washington City, Cumberland, Parkersburg, Cincinnati, St. Louis, Mexico, Kansas City, St. Josephs, Omaha, Ogden, SALT LAKE CITY, Sacramento, SAN FRANCISCO, returning to Omaha, Chicago, Detroit, Niagara Falls, Buffalo, and by Erie Railway to Elmira and New York, or vice versa.
First class $277.85

ROUTE 875.—NEW YORK TO DENVER, SALT LAKE, SAN FRANCISCO, and return, via Philadelphia, Baltimore, Washington City, Cumberland, Parkersburg, Cincinnati, St. Louis, Mexico, Kansas City, DENVER, Cheyenne, Ogden, SALT LAKE CITY, Sacramento, SAN FRANCISCO, and back to Cheyenne, Omaha, Chicago, Kalamazoo, Detroit, Niagara Falls, Rochester, Syracuse, Albany, and down Hudson (by rail or boat) to New York, or from Niagara Falls by Erie Railway to Buffalo, Elmira, and New York.
First class $291.85

ROUTE 876.—NEW YORK TO SALT LAKE, SAN FRANCISCO, DENVER, and return, via Hudson River (rail or boat) to Albany, rail to Syracuse, Rochester, Niagara Falls, Hamilton, Detroit, Chicago, Omaha, SALT LAKE CITY, Sacramento, SAN FRANCISCO, returning to Cheyenne, DENVER, Kansas City, Mexico, Bloomington, Chicago, Detroit, Niagara Falls, Buffalo, and Erie Railway to New York, or vice versa.
First class $291.55

ROUTE 877.—NEW YORK TO DENVER, SALT LAKE, SAN FRANCISCO, and return, via rail to Philadelphia, Pittsburg, Columbus, Cincinnati, Vincennes, St. Louis, Mexico, Kansas City, DENVER, Cheyenne, Ogden, SALT LAKE CITY, Sacramento, SAN FRANCISCO, returning to Omaha, Chicago, Kalamazoo, Detroit, Niagara Falls, Rochester, Syracuse, Albany, and down the Hudson (by rail or boat) to New York, or from Niagara Falls by Erie Railway to Elmira and New York.
First class $291.30

ROUTE 878.—NEW YORK TO SALT LAKE, SAN FRANCISCO, and return, via Philadelphia, Baltimore, Washington City, Alexandria, Gordonsville, Staunton, White Sulphur Springs, Huntington, steamer down the Ohio River to Cincinnati, rail to Covington, Louisville, Jeffersonville, Vincennes, St. Louis, Mexico, Kansas City, across the Buffalo Plains to Denver, Cheyenne, Ogden, SALT LAKE, Sacramento, SAN FRANCISCO, returning to Omaha, Chicago, Detroit, Niagara Falls, Syracuse, Albany, and down Hudson to New York by rail or boat, or from Niagara Falls to Buffalo and Elmira, by Erie Railway to New York.
First class $291.85

ROUTE 879.—NEW YORK TO DENVER, SALT LAKE, SAN FRAN-

CISCO, and return, *via* Philadelphia, Harrisburg, Pittsburg, Fort Wayne, Chicago, Bloomington, Mexico, Kansas City, DENVER, Cheyenne, Ogden, SALT LAKE, Sacramento, SAN FRANCISCO, Omaha, Chicago, Detroit, Niagara Falls, New York, either by the Erie Railway or the New York Central to Albany, and down the Hudson by rail or boat.

First class $290.45

ROUTE 880.—NEW YORK TO DENVER, SALT LAKE, SAN FRANCISCO, and return, same as above to SAN FRANCISCO, and back to Omaha, St. Josephs, Leavenworth, Kansas City, Mexico, St. Louis, Vincennes, Cincinnati, Parkersburg, Cumberland, Washington City, Baltimore, Philadelphia, and New York.

First class $288.80

ROUTE 881.—NEW YORK TO SAN FRANCISCO, SALT LAKE, MONTREAL, and return, *via* N. Y. C. or Erie Railway to Niagara Falls, Detroit, Chicago, Omaha, Ogden, SALT LAKE CITY, Sacramento, SAN FRANCISCO, and back to Omaha, Chicago, Detroit, Toronto, Lake Ontario, 1000 Islands, Rapids of St. Lawrence, MONTREAL, Lake Champlain, Saratoga, Albany, and down Hudson (by rail or boat) to New York.

First class $294.45

ROUTE 882.—NEW YORK TO SAN FRANCISCO, MONTREAL, and return, *via* Philadelphia, Baltimore, Washington City, Parkersburg, Cincinnati, St. Louis, Kansas City, Omaha, Salt Lake City, SAN FRANCISCO, Omaha, Chicago, Detroit, Niagara Falls, Toronto, 1000 Islands, Rapids of St. Lawrence, MONTREAL, Lake Champlain, Saratoga, Albany, and down Hudson (by rail or boat) to New York.

First class $297.35

ROUTE 883.—NEW YORK TO DENVER, SAN FRANCISCO, MONTREAL, an return, *via* rail to Philadelphia, Baltimore, Washington, Parkersburg, Cincinnati, St. Louis, Kansas City, over the great Buffalo Plains to DENVER, Cheyenne, Salt Lake City, SAN FRANCISCO, Omaha, Chicago, Detroit, Niagara Falls, Toronto, 1000 Islands, Rapids of St. Lawrence, MONTREAL, Lake Champlain, Saratoga, Albany, and down Hudson (by rail or boat) to New York.

First class $311.35

ROUTE 884.—NEW YORK TO DENVER, SAN FRANCISCO, MONTREAL, QUEBEC, BOSTON, and return, *via* same route as above to SAN FRANCISCO, returning to Omaha, Chicago, Detroit, Niagara Falls, Toronto, 1000 Islands, Rapids of St. Lawrence, MONTREAL, QUEBEC, Portland, BOSTON, Newport or Fall River, and steamer to New York.

First class $315.65

ROUTE 885.—NEW YORK TO SAN FRANCISCO, MONTREAL, QUEBEC, BOSTON, and return, *via* Hudson River to Albany (rail or boat), rail to Niagara Falls, Hamilton, Detroit, Chicago, Omaha, Salt Lake City, SAN FRANCISCO, returning direct to Omaha, Chicago, Detroit, Toronto, 1000 Island, Rapids of St. Lawrence, MONTREAL, QUEBEC, Portland, BOSTON, Fall River (or Newport), and Sound steamer to New York.

First class $301.75

ROUTE 886,—NEW YORK TO SAN FRANCISCO, MONTREAL, QUEBEC, and return, *via* Philadelphia, Baltimore, Washington City, Cumberland, Cincinnati, St. Louis, Kansas City, across the great Buffalo Plains to Denver, Cheyenne, Salt Lake City, Sacramento, SAN FRANCISCO, Omaha, Chicago, Detroit, Niagara Falls, Toronto, 1000 Islands, Rapids of St. Lawrence, MONTREAL, Quebec, Portland, Boston, Fall River, and Sound steamer to New York.

First class $315.65

ROUTE 887.—NEW YORK TO SAN FRANCISCO, THE YOSEMITE VALLEY, and return, *via* Philadelphia, Baltimore, Washington City, Parkersburg, Cincinnati, Louisville, St. Louis, Mexico, Kansas City, Denver, Cheyenne, Ogden, SALT LAKE CITY, Sacramento, San Francisco, Lathrop, Merced, stage to Coultersville, and horseback three miles to THE YOSEMITE, returning *via* Inspiration Point, Sentinel Dome, Mariposa, Grove of Big Trees, Clarks, Hatch's to Merced, and rail to Lathrop, Cheyenne, Omaha, Chicago, Detroit, Niagara Falls, Albany, and down the Hudson (by rail or boat) to New York, or by Erie Railway from Niagara Falls to Buffalo, Elmira, and New York.

First class . . . . r . . . $356.75

ROUTE 888.—NEW YORK TO SAN FRANCISCO, THE YOSEMITE VALLEY, and return, *via* Hudson River to Albany (rail or boat), rail to Niagara Falls, Detroit, Chicago, Omaha, Salt Lake City, Sacramento, SAN FRANCISCO, Merced, THE YOSEMITE VALLEY, *via* Coultersville, and back to Merced *via* Mariposa, thence to Lathrop, Ogden, Omaha, Chicago, Detroit, Niagara Falls, Buffalo, Elmira, New York, or *vice versa*.

First class $340.95

ROUTE 889.—NEW YORK TO SAN FRANCISCO, THE YOSEMITE, CHICAGO, MONTREAL, and return, *via* Philadelphia, Baltimore, Washington City, Parkersburg, Cincinnati, Louisville, St. Louis, Kansas City, Denver, Cheyenne, Ogden, Salt Lake City, Sacramento, SAN FRANCISCO, Lathrop, Merced, THE YOSEMITE, into the Valley one route and back another, Lathrop, Omaha, Chicago, Detroit, London, Niagara Falls, Toronto, Lake Ontario, 1000 Islands, Rapids of St. Lawrence, Montreal Quebec, White Mountains, Boston, and Fall River Line of steamers to New York.

First class $378.90

ROUTE 890.—NEW YORK TO SAN FRANCISCO, YOSEMITE, CHICAGO, MONTREAL, and return, *via* same as above to Kansas City, thence to Omaha, Ogden, Salt Lake City, SAN FRANCISCO, returning to Lathrop, Merced, into the Yosemite Valley, by Coultersville, and back by Mariposa, Lathrop, Ogden, Omaha, Chicago, Detroit, Niagara Falls, Toronto, Kingston, Lake Ontario, 1000 Islands, Rapids of St. Lawrence, Montreal, Rouse's Point, Lake Champlain, Saratoga, Albany, and by rail or boat to New York.

First class $359.00

ROUTE 891.—NEW YORK TO SAN FRANCISCO, THE YOSEMITE, THE GEYSERS, and return, *via* rail to Philadelphia, Baltimore, Washington City, Parkersburg, Cincinnati, Louisville, St. Louis, Mexico, Kansas City, Omaha, Ogden, Salt Lake City, Sacramento, SAN FRANCISCO, THE GEYSERS, and back to San Francisco, rail to Lathrop, Merced, The Yosemite Valley, and back to Merced, Lathrop, Omaha, Chicago, Detroit, Niagara Falls, Albany, and down the Hudson (by rail or boat) to New York, or from Niagara Falls to Buffalo, and New York by the Erie R. W.

First class $358.25

ROUTE 892.—NEW YORK TO SAN FRANCISCO, THE YOSEMITE, THE GEYSERS, CHICAGO, MONTREAL, QUEBEC, and return, *via* same route as above to SAN FRANCISCO, to the Geysers, and back to San Francisco, rail to Lathrop, Merced, and stage to the YOSEMITE VALLEY, and back to Merced, rail to Lathrop, Omaha, Chicago, Detroit, Niagara Falls, Toronto, Lake Ontario, 1000 Islands, Rapids of the St. Lawrence, Montreal, Quebec, White Mountains, Boston, and Sound steamer to New York.

First class . . . . . . , . . $375.90

ROUTE 893.—NEW YORK TO SAN FRANCISCO, THE GEYSERS, THE YOSEMITE VALLEY, MONTREAL, and return, *via* Philadelphia, Baltimore, Washington City, Gordonsville, White Sulphur Springs, West Virginia to Huntington, steamer down the Ohio to Cincinnati, rail to Louisville, St. Louis Kansas City, over the great Buffalo Plains to Denver, Cheyenne, Ogden,

Salt Lake City, Sacramento, SAN FRANCISCO, THE GEYSERS, and back to San Francisco, rail to Lathrop, Merced, stage and horseback into the Yosemite, by Coultersville, and out by Mariposa, Merced, Lathrop, Omaha, Chicago, Detroit, Niagara Falls, Toronto, Lake Ontario, 1000 Islands, Rapids of St. Lawrence, Montreal, Quebec, White Mountains, Boston, and Sound steamer *via* Newport to New York.

First class $397.00

ROUTE 894.—NEW YORK TO SAN FRANCISCO, THE GEYSERS, THE YOSEMITE, MONTREAL, and return, *via* Hudson River to Albany (rail or boat), rail to Niagara Falls, or by Erie Railway to Niagara Falls, Detroit, Chicago, Omaha, Salt Lake City, SAN FRANCISCO, THE GEYSERS, and back to San Francisco, Lathrop, Merced, THE YOSEMITE VALLEY, and back to Merced, rail to Lathrop, Omaha, Chicago, Detroit, Niagara Falls, Toronto, Lake Ontario, 1000 Islands, Rapids of St. Lawrence, MONTREAL, Quebec, White Mountains, Boston, and Fall River steamer to New York.

First class $378.60

ROUTE 895.—NEW YORK TO SAN FRANCISCO, THE GEYSERS, THE YOSEMITE, MONTREAL, and return, *via* rail to Philadelphia, Baltimore, Washington City, Parkersburg, Cincinnati, Louisville, St. Louis, Kansas City, Denver, Cheyenne, Ogden, Salt Lake City, Sacramento, SAN FRANCISCO, boat to Donahau, rail to Cloverdale, and stage to Geysers, and back to Cloverdale, rail and boat to San Francisco, rail to Lathrop, Merced, and stage into the YOSEMITE VALLEY, and back to Merced, rail to Lathrop, Ogden, Omaha, Chicago, Detroit, Niagara Falls, Toronto, Lake Ontario, 1000 Islands, Rapids of St. Lawrence, Montreal, Quebec, White Mountains, Boston, and Fall River steamer to New York. ·

First class $394.90

Tours to St. Paul, the North West, Combining the Mississippi River.

ROUTE 897.—NEW YORK TO ST. PAUL and return, *via* Hudson River (rail or boat) to Albany, rail to Syracuse, Rochester, Niagara Falls, Detroit, Chicago, Beloit, Madison, Black River Falls, ST. PAUL, returning the same way to Chicago, thence to Niagara Falls, and by Erie Railway to New York, or *vice versa*.

First class $72.70

ROUTE 897.—NEW YORK TO ST. PAUL and return, *via* Philadelphia, Harrisburg, Pittsburg, Fort Wayne, Chicago, Beloit, Madison, ST. PAUL, returning same route to Chicago, thence to Detroit, Hamilton, Niagara Falls, Rochester, Albany, and down Hudson (by rail or boat) to New York.

First class $70.05

ROUTE 898.—NEW YORK TO ST. PAUL and return, *via* same as above to ST. PAUL, and back to Niagara Falls, thence by Erie Railway to Buffalo, Elmira, and New York.

First class $70.05

ROUTE 899.—NEW YORK TO ST. PAUL, ST. LOUIS, and return, *via* Hudson River (rail or boat) to Albany, rail to Rochester, Niagara Falls, Hamilton, Detroit, Chicago, Beloit, Madison, ST. PAUL, returning to Chicago, thence rail to Bloomington, Springfield, ST. LOUIS, Vincennes, Cincinnati, Parkersburg, Cumberland, Washington City, Baltimore, Philadelphia, and New York, or *vice versa*.

First class $81.80

ROUTE 900.—NEW YORK TO ST. PAUL, ST. LOUIS, and return, *via* Philadelphia, Harrisburg, Pittsburg, Fort Wayne, Chicago, Beloit, Madison, ST. PAUL, back same way to Chicago, thence Bloomington, Springfield, ST. LOUIS, Cincinnati, Parkersburg, Cumberland, Washington City, Baltimore, Philadelphia, and New York.
First class $79.15

ROUTE 901.—NEW YORK TO ST. PAUL, ST. LOUIS, and return, *via* Erie Railway to Elmira, Buffalo, Niagara Falls, Hamilton, Detroit, Chicago, Beloit, Madison, ST. PAUL, and back to New York same as above.
First class $81.80

ROUTE 902.—NEW YORK TO ST. PAUL, ST. LOUIS and return, *via* Hudson River (rail or boat) to Albany, or Erie Railway to Niagara Falls, Detroit, Chicago, Beloit, Madison, ST. PAUL, steamer down the Mississippi (meals and staterooms included) to Dubuque, Davenport, Keokuk, ST. LOUIS, rail to Cincinnati, Parkersburg, Cumberland, Washington, Baltimore, Philadelphia, New York, or *vice versa*.
First class $74.70

ROUTE 903.—NEW YORK TO ST. PAUL, ST. LOUIS and return, *via* Philadelphia, Pittsburg, Fort Wayne, Chicago, Beloit, Madison, ST. PAUL, steamer down the Missippi River to ST. LOUIS (meals and staterooms included), rail to Cincinnati, Parkersburg, Cumberland, Washington City, Baltimore, Philadelphia, and New York, or *vice versa*.
First class $72.05

ROUTE 904.—NEW YORK TO ST. LOUIS, ST. PAUL and return, *via* Hudson River (rail or boat) to Albany, or Erie Railway to Niagara Falls, Hamilton, Detroit, Chicago, Springfield, ST. LOUIS, steamer up the Mississippi River to ST. PAUL (meals and staterooms included), rail to Madison, Beloit, Chicago, Detroit, Niagara Falls, Albany, New York, or *vice versa*.
First class $77.80

Tours to the Northern Lakes, Duluth, Lake Superior, Lake Michigan, Lake Erie, Lake Huron, Georgian Bay, &c.

MEALS AND STATEROOMS ON STEAMERS INCLUDED.

ROUTE 905.—NEW YORK TO DETROIT and return, *via* Erie or New York Central Railroad to Buffalo, Ward's Line of Steamers to Cleveland, Michigan Central Railroad Steamers to DETROIT, back to Niagara Falls, Albany, and down the Hudson to New York, or *vice versa*.
First class · · · · · · $30.50

ROUTE 906.—NEW YORK TO SAULT ST. MARIE and return, *via* Hudson River (rail or boat) to Albany, rail to Niagara Falls, Hamilton, Detroit, Ward's Line of steamers to SAULT ST. MARIE, returning same way to Niagara Falls, thence by either Erie or New York Central Railroad to New York.
First class · · · · · · $49.50

ROUTE 907.—NEW YORK TO SAULT ST. MARIE and return, *via* Erie or New York Central Railroad to Buffalo, thence by Ward's Line of Steamers to Cleveland, Detroit, SAULT ST. MARIE, returning the same way.
First class · · · · · · $44.50

ROUTE 908.—NEW YORK TO SAULT ST. MARIE and return, *via* Erie or New York Central Railroad to Buffalo, Ward's Line to Cleveland, Detroit,

SAULT ST. MARIE, returning by steamer to Detroit, rail to Niagara Falls, Albany, and down the Hudson to New York, or *vice versa*.
First class - - - - - - - $47.00

ROUTE 909.—NEW YORK TO SAULT ST. MARIE and return, *via* Hudson River (rail or boat) to Albany, rail to Syracuse, Buffalo (or by Erie Railway direct to Buffalo), thence by Ward's line of steamers (meals and staterooms included) to Cleveland, Detroit, SAULT ST. MARIE, returning by Collingwood line through Georgian Bay, Collingwood, Toronto, Niagara Falls, and back to New York by Erie or New York Centra. Railway, or *vice versa*.
First class - - - - - - - $44.05

ROUTE 910.—NEW YORK TO SAULT ST. MARIE and return, *via* Hudson River or Erie Railway to Niagara Falls, rail to Toronto, Collingwood, and steamer through Georgian Bay to SAULT ST. MARIE, returning the same way.
First class - - - - - - - $43.60

ROUTE 911.—NEW YORK TO MARQUETTE and return, *via* New York Central or Erie Railway to Buffalo, Ward's Line of Lake Superior Steamers to Cleveland, Detroit, Sault St. Marie, MARQUETTE, returning to Sault St. Marie, then by steamer of Collingwood Line to Collingwood, rail to Toronto, Niagara Falls, and back to New York by Erie or New York Central Railroad, or *vice versa*.
First class - - - - - - - $54.05

ROUTE 912.—NEW YORK TO CHICAGO, *via* Hudson River steamer to Albany, and rail to Buffalo, or *via* rail direct either Erie Railway or New York Central Railroad to Buffalo, thence by steamer sailing every evening (except Sunday and Monday), at 7 P. M., to Erie, Cleveland, Detroit, Straits of Mackinac and Lake Michigan, Milwaukee, Chicago, including meals and staterooms on Lake steamers, or *vice versa*.
First class - - - - - - - - $23.25

ROUTE 913.—NEW YORK TO CHICAGO and return, *via* Hudson River steamer to Albany, thence by rail to Buffalo, thence by Lake steamer, sailing every evening (except Sunday and Monday), at 7 P. M., to Erie, Cleveland, Detroit, Straits of Mackinac, Milwaukee, CHICAGO, returning same way to Buffalo, thence by Erie Railway to New York, or *vice versa*. Meals and staterooms on steamer included.
First class - - - - - - - $45.50

ROUTE 914.—NEW YORK TO CHICAGO and return, *via* Hudson River steamer to Albany, thence rail to Troy, Saratoga, Schenectady, Buffalo, thence boat over Lakes Erie and Huron, through the Straits, and *via* Lake Machingi to CHICAGO, returning same way to Buffalo, thence to New York either *via* Erie or New York Central Railroad, or *vice versa*.
First class - - - - - - - $48.25

ROUTE 915.—NEW YORK TO CHICAGO and return, *via* rail to Philadelphia, Pittsburg, Fort Wayne, CHICAGO, returning by steamer of the Union Line to Milwaukee, Straits of Mackinac, Detroit, Buffalo, thence to New York by Erie or New York Central Railroad.
First class - - - - - - - $42.00

ROUTE 916.—NEW YORK TO ST. LOUIS, *via* Hudson River steamers to Albany, rail to Troy, Saratoga, Buffalo, steamer to Erie, Cleveland, Detroit, Straits of Mackinac, Milwaukee, Chicago, thence rail to ST. LOUIS. Meals and staterooms on Lake boats included.
First class - - - - - - - $31.00

ROUTE 917.—NEW YORK TO KANSAS CITY, *via* Hudson River to Albany, Troy, rail to Saratoga, Buffalo, steamer to Erie, Cleveland, Detroit, Straits of Mackinac, Milwaukee, Chicago, rail *via* Mexico to Kansas City. Meals and staterooms on Lake boats included.
First class - - - ; ! - - - $36.00

ROUTE 918.—NEW YORK TO DULUTH and return, *via* Hudson River to Albany (rail or boat), rail to Syracuse, Rochester, Niagara Falls, Suspension Bridge, Toronto, Collingwood, thence by steamer sailing every Tuesday and Friday to Georgian Bay, Killarney, Sault St. Marie, along the north shore of Lake Superior, Nipegon Bay, Thunder Bay, Fort William, Silver Island, DU-LUTH, returning to Sault St. Marie, Collingwood, Toronto, Kingston, across Lake Ontario to Cape Vincent, Rome, Albany, and down Hudson to New York.

First class $79.37

ROUTE 919.—NEW YORK TO DULUTH and return, *via* Erie Railway to Buffalo, Niagara Falls, Toronto, Collingwood, and steamer sailing every Tuesday and Friday for Georgian Bay, Killarney, Bruce Mines, Bear Lake, Sault St. Marie (steamer stops 6 hours, giving time for trout fishing, shooting, the Rapids in canoes), through Lake Superior to Nipegon Bay (celebrated for fine fishing), Silver Island, Thunder Bay, DULUTH, returning to Sault St. Marie, Collingwood, Toronto, Niagara Falls, Rochester, Syracuse, Albany, and down the Hudson (by rail or boat) to New York, or *vice versa*.

First class $74.30

ROUTE 920.—NEW YORK TO DULUTH and return, *via* Hudson River (rail or boat) to Albany, rail to Syracuse, Rochester, Niagara Falls, Toronto, Collingwood, and steamer sailing every Tuesday and Friday for Georgian Bay, Killarney, Sault St. Marie, Lake Superior, Nipegon Bay, Silver Island, Fort William, DULUTH, returning by steamer to Sault St. Marie, Collingwood, Toronto, Lake Ontario, 1000 Islands, Rapids of St. Lawrence, Montreal, Rouse's Point, Lake Champlain, Saratoga, Albany, and down the Hudson to New York.

First class $88.50

ROUTE 921.—NEW YORK TO DULUTH, MONTREAL, and return, same as above to Duluth, returning to Toronto, and by steamer 1000 Islands, Rapids of St. Lawrence) MONTREAL, Quebec, White Mountains, Boston, Fall River, and steamer to New York.

First class $94.45

ROUTE 922.—NEW YORK TO DULUTH and return, *via* Erie or New York Central Railroad to Buffalo, Ward's Line of Steamers to Cleveland, Detroit, Sault St. Marie, Marquette, Copper Harbor, Ontonagon, DULUTH, returning the same way to Buffalo, thence by Erie or New York Central Railroad to New York.

First class - - - - - - $72.50

ROUTE 923.—NEW YORK TO DULUTH and return, *via* Hudson River (rail or boat) to Albany, rail to Niagara Falls, Toronto, Collingwood, steamer to Sault St. Marie, Nipejon, Thunder Bay, Fort Wheelan, Silver Island, DULUTH, returning by Ward's Line of Steamers to Ontonagon, Eagle Harbor, Copper Harbor, Marquette, Sault St. Marie, Detroit, Cleveland, Buffalo, and rail to New York by Erie or New York Central Railroad, or *vice versa*.

First class - - - - - $74.50

ROUTE 924.—NEW YORK TO DULUTH and return, *via* Hudson River (rail or boat) to Albany, rail to Rome, Cape Vincent, steamer on Lake Ontario to Kingston, rail to Toronto, Collingwood, steamer to Sault St. Marie, Nipejon, Thunder Bay, Fort William, Silver Island, DULUTH, returning by Ward's Line of Steamers to Ontonagon, Eagle Harbor, Copper Harbor, Marquette, Sault St. Marie, Detroit, rail to Suspension Bridge, Niagara Falls, and back to New York by Erie or New York Central Railroad, or *vice versa*.

First class - - - - - $81.65

ROUTE 925.—NEW YORK TO CHICAGO, ST. PAUL, DULUTH, LAKE SUPERIOR and return, *via* Hudson River (rail or boat) to Albany, rail to Buffalo (or by Erie Railway to Buffalo,) steamer sailing every evening (except Sunday) to Detroit, Straits of Mackinac, Milwaukee, CHICAGO, rail to Madison,

St. Paul, Duluth, and steamer to Silver Island, Thunder Bay, Sault St. Marie, Collingwood, Toronto, Niagara Falls, thence to New York, or *vice versa*.

First class - - - - - - - $82.65

ROUTE 926.—NEW YORK TO CHICAGO, ST. PAUL, DULUTH, LAKE SUPERIOR and return, *via* Hudson River (rail or boat) to Albany, or by Erie Railway to Niagara Falls, Detroit, CHICAGO, Madison, ST. PAUL, DULUTH, steamer to Ontonagon, Copper Harbor, Marquette, Sault St. Marie, Detroit, Cleveland, Buffalo, and by Erie or New York Central Railroad back to New York, or *vice versa*.

First class - - - - - - - - - $79.75

ROUTE 927.—NEW YORK TO CHICAGO, ST. PAUL, DULUTH, LAKE SUPERIOR and return, *via* Hudson River (rail or boat) to Albany, Niagara Falls (or by Erie Railway direct), Detroit, CHICAGO, Madison, ST. PAUL, DULUTH, steamer of Collingwood Line to Thunder Bay, Sault St. Marie, through the Georgian Bay to Collingwood, rail to Toronto, Niagara Falls, and by Erie or New York Central Railroad to New York, or *vice versa*.

First class - - - - - - - - - $79.75

ROUTE 928.—NEW YORK TO CHICAGO, ST. PAUL, DULUTH, LAKE SUPERIOR and return, *via* rail Philadelphia, Pittsburg, Fort Wayne, CHICAGO, ST. PAUL, DULUTH, and steamer to Ontonagon, Copper Harbor, Marquette, Sault St. Marie, Detroit, Cleveland, Buffalo, and by Erie or New York Central Railroad back to New York

First class - - - - - - - - $76.90

ROUTE 929.—NEW YORK TO CHICAGO, ST. PAUL, DULUTH, LAKE SUPERIOR and return, *via* rail to Philadelphia, Pittsburg, Fort Wayne, CHICAGO, Madison, ST. PAUL, DULUTH, and steamer to Silver Island, Thunder Bay Sault St. Marie, through Georgian Bay to Collingwood, rail to Toronto, Niagara Falls, and thence to New York by either Erie or New York Central Railroad.

First class - - - - - - - $76.90

ROUTE 930.—NEW YORK TO ST. LOUIS, MISSISSIPPI RIVER, ST. PAUL, DULUTH, LAKE SUPERIOR and return, *via* Philadelphia, Baltimore, Washington City, Parkersburg, Cincinnati, ST. LOUIS, steamer up the Mississippi River (meals and state-rooms included) to Keokuk, Davenport, ST. PAUL, rail to Duluth, steamer to Thunder Bay, Silver Island, Sault St. Marie, through Georgian Bay to Collingwood, rail to Toronto, Niagara Falls, and by Erie or New York Central R.R. back to New York, or *vice versa*.

First class - - - - - $83.75

ROUTE 931.—NEW YORK TO ST. LOUIS, MISSISSIPPI RIVER, ST. PAUL, DULUTH, LAKE SUPERIOR, and return, *via* same route as above to St. Paul and Duluth, thence by steamer to Ontonagon, Copper Harbor, Marquette, Sault St. Marie, Detroit, Cleveland, Buffalo, thence by Erie or New York Central R.R. to New York, or *vice versa*.

First class - - - - - $83.75

ROUTE 932.—NEW YORK TO CHICAGO, ST. LOUIS, MISSISSIPPI RIVER, ST. PAUL, DULUTH, LAKE SUPERIOR, and return, *via* Hudson River (rail or boat) to Albany. Buffalo (or Erie Railway direct), steamer to Detroit, Straits of Mackanac, Milwaukie. Chicago, rail to St. Louis, steamer up the Mississippi to Keokuk, Davenport, ST. PAUL, Duluth, steamer to Thunder Bay, Sault St. Marie, through Georgian Bay, to Collingwood, rail to Toronto, Niagara Falls, thence by Erie or New York Central back to New York, or *vice versa*.

First class • • • - • • $89.70

TOURS TO NIAGARA FALLS.

ROUTE 933.—NEW YORK TO NIAGARA FALLS and return, *via* Hudson River (rail or boat) to Albany, rail to Syracuse, Rochester, NIAGARA FALLS, returning to Buffalo, Attica, Elmira, New York, or *vice versa.*
First class $17.50

ROUTE 934.—NEW YORK TO NIAGARA FALLS and return, *via* day or night boat on Hudson to Albany, rail to Syracuse, Rochester, NIAGARA FALLS, returning the same way.
First class $16.30

ROUTE 935.—NEW YORK TO NIAGARA FALLS and return, *via* day or night steamer to Albany, rail to Syracuse, Rochester, NIAGARA FALLS, returning by Erie Railway to Buffalo, Elmira and New York, or *vice versa.*
First class $17.50

ROUTE 936.—NEW YORK TO NIAGARA FALLS and return, *via* Hudson River Railroad to Albany, Syracuse, Rochester, NIAGARA FALLS, returning the same way to Albany, thence down the Hudson by day or night boat, or *vice versa.*
First class $17.50

ROUTE 937.—NEW YORK TO NIAGARA FALLS and return, *via* Erie or New York Central Railroad in both directions.
First class $17.50

ROUTE 938.—NEW YORK TO NIAGARA FALLS and return, *via* Erie Railroad to Buffalo and Niagara Falls, and return *via* Albany and Hudson River steamers to New York.
First class $17.50

ROUTE 939.—NEW YORK TO NIAGARA FALLS and return, *via* Erie Railroad to Niagara Falls, and return *via* Erie Railroad to Binghampton, Albany, Hudson River steamers to New York.
First class $17.50

ROUTE 940.—NEW YORK TO NIAGARA FALLS, *via* Hudson River steamer to Albany, Troy, rail to Schenectady, Saratoga, thence to Niagara Falls.
First class $10.70

ROUTE 941.—NEW YORK TO NIAGARA FALLS and return, *via* rail or steamer on Hudson River to Albany, thence rail to NIAGARA FALLS, returning by Erie Railroad to Waverly, Bethlehem, Philadelphia, and back to New York.
First class $21.25

ROUTE 942.—NEW YORK TO NIAGARA FALLS and return, *via* Erie Railroad to Elmira, Canandaigua, NIAGARA FALLS, returning direct *via* Erie Railroad.
First class . . . $18.00

ROUTE 943.—NEW YORK TO NIAGARA FALLS and return, *via* Erie Railroad to Elmira, Buffalo, Niagara Falls, returning *via* N. Y. C. Railroad to Geneva, steamer on Seneca Lake to Watkins (for the Glen), rail to Elmira, and back to New York.
First class . . . $18.50

ROUTE 944.—NEW YORK TO NIAGARA FALLS and return, *via* Erie Railroad to Elmira, Buffalo, NIAGARA FALLS, Albany, Saratoga, Albany and Hudson River steamer to New York.
First class $19.30

ROUTE 945.—NEW YORK TO NIAGARA FALLS and return, *via* Hudson River steamer to Albany, rail to Saratoga, Schenectady, NIAGARA FALLS, returning *via* Buffalo, Elmira, and back to New York.
First class $18.55

ROUTE 946.—NEW YORK TO NIAGARA FALLS and return, via Erie Railroad to Elmira, Buffalo, NIAGARA FALLS, Utica, Richfield Springs, steamer on Otsego Lake to Cooperstown, rail to Albany, and steamer down the Hudson to New York.

First class $19.25

ROUTE 947.—NEW YORK TO NIAGARA FALLS and return, via Hudson River steamers to Albany, rail to Sharon Springs and Cherry Valley, stage and boat on Otsego Lake to Cooperstown and Richfield Springs, rail to Utica, NIAGARA FALLS, Buffalo, Elmira, New York.

First class $19.55

ROUTE 948.—NEW YORK TO NIAGARA FALLS and return, via Erie Railroad to Elmira, Buffalo, NIAGARA FALLS, Cayuga, steamer on Cayuga Lake to Ithaca, rail to Owego and New York.

First class $18.40

ROUTE 949.—NEW YORK TO NIAGARA FALLS and return, via Erie Railroad to Niagara Falls, Waverly, Mauch Chunk, New York.

First class $18.15

ROUTE 950.—NEW YORK TO NIAGARA FALLS and return, via Erie Railroad, Elmira, Buffalo to NIAGARA FALLS, Syracuse, Sandy Creek, Cape Vincent, steamer on Lake Ontario to Alexandria Bay and back, rail to Sandy Creek, Syracuse, Binghampton, New York.

First class $24.85

ROUTE 951.—NEW YORK TO NIAGARA FALLS and return, via Erie Railroad, Elmira, Buffalo, NIAGARA FALLS, Syracuse, Sandy Creek, Cape Vincent, steamer on Lake Ontario to Alexandria Bay and back to Cape Vincent, rail to Rome, Albany, and steamer down Hudson River to New York.

First class $23.15

ROUTE 952.—NEW YORK TO NIAGARA FALLS and return, via Erie Railroad, Elmira, WATKINS, steamer on Seneca Lake to Geneva, rail to NIAGARA FALLS, returning by Erie Railway to New York.

First class $18.50

ROUTE 953.—NEW YORK TO NIAGARA FALLS via Hudson River (rail or boat) to Albany, rail to Cooperstown, steamer on Otsego Lake, and stage to Richfield Springs, rail to Utica and NIAGARA FALLS.

First class - - - - - - $11.75

ROUTE 954.—NEW YORK TO RITCHFIELD SPRINGS, NIAGARA FALLS and return, same as above to Niagara, returning by New York Central to Albany, thence rail or boat to New York.

First class - - - - - - $20.00

ROUTE 955.—NEW YORK TO WATKINS GLEN, NIAGARA FALLS and return, via Hudson River (rail or boat) to Albany, rail to Geneva, steamer to WATKINS, rail to Canandaigua, NIAGARA FALLS, Albany, New York.

First class - - - - - - $19.00

ROUTE 956.—NEW YORK TO WATKINS GLEN, NIAGARA FALLS and return, via Hudson River (rail or boat) to Albany, rail to Geneva, steamer to WATKINS, and back to Geneva, rail to NIAGARA FALLS, returning to Albany and New York.

First class - - - - - - $19.00

TOURS TO SARATOGA, ALEXANDRIA BAY (1000 ISLANDS), CANADA, MONTREAL, BOSTON, LAKE CHAMPLAIN, LAKE GEORGE.

ROUTE 957.—NEW YORK TO SARATOGA and return, *via* Hudson River Railroad to Troy, Saratoga, and back the same way.

First class $8.40

ROUTE 958.—NEW YORK TO SARATOGA and return, *via* day or night boat to Albany, rail to Saratoga, and back same way.

First class . . . . - . $6.60

ROUTE 959.—NEW YORK TO ALBANY and return, up the Hudson by day boat, returning by day or night boat.

First class $4.00

ROUTE 960.—NEW YORK TO HOWE'S CAVE and return, *via* Hudson River (day or night boat) to Albany, thence by rail to HOWE'S CAVE, returning the same way.

First class - - - - - - - - - $6.60

ROUTE 961.—NEW YORK TO COOPERSTOWN and return, *via* Hudson River (day or night boat) to Albany, rail to COOPERSTOWN, and returning same way.

First class - - - - - - - - - $10.85

ROUTE 962.—NEW YORK TO COOPERSTOWN and return, *via* Hudson River Railroad to Albany, rail to COOPERSTOWN, and back the same way to Albany, thence rail or boat to New York.

First class - - - - - - - - - $13.05

ROUTE 963.—NEW YORK TO RICHFIELD SPRINGS and return, *via* Hudson River steamer to Albany, rail to Utica, RICHFIELD SPRINGS, steamer on Otsego Lake to Cooperstown, rail to Binghamton and New York.

First class $12.30

ROUTE 964.—NEW YORK TO RICHFIELD SPRINGS and return, *via* Hudson River (day or night boat) to Albany, rail to Cooperstown, and steamer on Otsego Lake to RICHFIELD SPRINGS, returning same way.

First class - - - - - - - - - $13.35

ROUTE 965.—NEW YORK TO RICHFIELD SPRINGS and return, *via* Hudson River Railroad to Albany, rail to Cooperstown, steamer on Otsego Lake to RICHFIELD SPRINGS, returning same way to Albany, thence rail or boat to New York.

First class - - - - - - - - - $15.85

ROUTE 966.—NEW YORK TO SHARON SPRINGS and return, *via* Hudson River day or night boat to Albany, and rail to SHARON SPRINGS, returning same way.

First class $8.00

ROUTE 967.—NEW YORK TO SHARON SPRINGS and return, *via* Hudson River Railroad to Albany, rail to Cobleskill and Sharon Springs, returning same way to Albany, and by day or night boat to New York, or *vice versa*.

First class $9.10

ROUTE 968.—NEW YORK TO TRENTON FALLS and return, *via* Erie Railway to Binghampton, Utica, TRENTON FALLS, Utica, Richfield Springs, steamer on Otsego Lake to Cooperstown, rail to Albany, and Hudson River steamer to New York.

First class $13.20

ROUTE 969.—NEW YORK TO TRENTON FALLS and return, *via* Hudson River steamer to Albany, rail to Utica, TRENTON FALLS, Utica, Binghampton, New York.

First class $10.85

ROUTE 970.—NEW YORK TO WATKIN'S GLEN and return, *via* Erie Railway to Elmira and WATKINS, returning the same way.
First class $13.00

ROUTE 971.—NEW YORK TO WATKIN'S GLEN and return, *via* Erie Railway to Elmira, WATKINS, steamer on Seneca Lake to Geneva, rail to Albany, and Hudson River steamer to New York.
First class $14.00

ROUTE 972.—NEW YORK TO WATKIN'S GLEN, *via* Hudson River (rail or boat), to Albany, rail to Geneva, steamer to WATKIN'S GLEN.
First class - - - - - - - - - $7.90

ROUTE 973.—NEW YORK TO WATKIN'S GLEN and return, *via* Hudson River (rail or boat) to Albany, rail to Geneva, steamer to WATKIN'S GLEN, returning same way.
First class - - - - - - - - $13.50

ROUTE 974.—NEW YORK TO SARATOGA, SHARON SPRINGS and return, *via* Hudson River (rail or boat), to Albany, rail to Troy, Saratoga, Schenectady. Palatine Bridge, coach to SHARON SPRINGS, rail to Albany, and down the Hudson (by rail or boat) to New York.
First class - - - - - - - - $11.75

ROUTE 975.—NEW YORK TO LAKE GEORGE and return, *via* Hudson River (rail or boat), to Albany, rail to Troy, Saratoga, Glen's Falls, stage to Caldwell, boat and stage to Ticonderoga, steamer to Whitehall, rail to Saratoga, Troy, New York.
First class - - - - - - - - - $15.00

ROUTE 976.—NEW YORK TO ALBANY, BOSTON, and return *via* day or night boat up the Hudson to Albany, rail to Springfield, Worcester, Boston, Fall River or Newport, and sound steamers back to New York, or *vice versa*.
First class $12.15

ROUTE 977.—NEW YORK TO SARATOGA, BOSTON, and return, *via* day or night boat on Hudson to Albany, rail to SARATOGA, Schenectady, Albany, Springfield, Worcester, Boston, Fall River or Newport, and Sound steamer to New York, or *vice versa*.
First class $14.55

ROUTE 978.—NEW YORK TO SARATOGA, BOSTON, and return, *via* Hudson River Railroad to Albany, Troy, SARATOGA, Schenectady, Albany, Springfield, Worcester, BOSTON, Fall River or Newport, and Sound steamer to New York, or *vice versa*.
First class . . . $15.45

ROUTE 979.—NEW YORK TO BOSTON, SARATOGA and return *via* Fall River Line to BOSTON, rail to Fitchburg, Bellow's Falls, Rutland, SARATOGA, Albany and steamer down the Hudson to New York, or *vice versa*.
First class - - - - - - - - , $13.95

ROTTE 980.—NEW YORK TO SARATOGA, BURLINGTON, BOSTON and return, *via* Hudson River (day or night boat), to Albany, rail to SARATOGA, Whitehall, steamer to BURLINGTON, rail to Bellow's Falls, Fitchburg, BOSTON, Fall River Line to New York.
First class - - - - - - - - $18.95

ROUTE 981.—NEW YORK TO LAKE GEORGE, BOSTON and return, *via* Hudson River (day or night boat), to Albany, rail to Saratoga, Glen's Falls, stage to Caldwell, boat on LAKE GEORGE, stage to Ticonderoga, boat to Burlington, rail to Fitchburg, BOSTON, and Fall River Line to New York.
First class - - - - - - - - $22.60

ROUTE 982.—NEW YORK TO ALEXANDRIA BAY and return, *via* Hudson River to Albany, rail to Rome, Cape Vincent, and then by steamer J. H. Kelly to ALEXANDRIA BAY, returning same way.
First class $17.00

44   COOK'S AMERICAN TOURS.

ROUTE 983.—NEW YORK TO ALEXANDRIA BAY and return, *via* Hudson River steamer or rail to Albany, rail to Rome, Cape Vincent, steamer to ALEXANDRIA BAY and back to Cape Vincent, rail to Rome, Watertown, Sandy Creek, Syracuse, Binghampton, New York, or back from Rome, same as outward.

First class $17.00

ROUTE 984.—NEW YORK TO TORONTO, *via* Hudson River to Albany and Troy, rail to Saratoga, Schenectady, Niagara Falls, Suspension Bridge, Hamilton, Toronto.

First class $13.25

ROUTE 985.—NEW YORK TO TORONTO, *via* Hudson River to Albany, rail to Rome, Cape Vincent, steamer on Lake Ontario to Kingston, rail to Toronto.

First class $14.80

ROUTE 986.—NEW YORK TO 1000 ISLANDS, MONTREAL, BOSTON and return, *via* Hudson River (rail or boat to Albany, rail to Rome, Cape Vincent, steamer to Alexandria Bay, Prescott, Rapids of St. Lawrence, MONTREAL, rail to Rouse's Point, steamer to Burlington, rail to Fitchburg, BOSTON, and Fall River Line to New York.

First class · · · · · · · · $29.65

ROUTE 987.—NEW YORK TO 1000 ISLANDS, MONTREAL, BOSTON and return, *via* same route as above to MONTREAL, thence rail to St. John's, St. Albans, stage to Bellow's Falls, rail to Fitchburg, BOSTON, and Fall River Line to New York.

First class · · · · · · · · $29.10

ROUTE 988.—NEW YORK TO CAPE VINCENT, NIAGARA FALLS, and return, *via* Hudson River to Albany, rail to Rome, Cape Vincent, steamer across Lake Ontario to Kingston, rail to Toronto, Suspension Bridge, NIAGARA FALLS, returning to New York by Erie or New York Central R.R.

First class $26.25

ROUTE 989.—NEW YORK TO OGDENSBURG, OTTAWA, MONTREAL, and return, *via* Hudson River to Albany, rail to Rome, Ogdensburg, ferry across St. Lawrence to Prescott, rail to Ottawa City, and steamer down Ottawa River to Lachine, Montreal, Rouse's Point, Lake Champlain, White Hall, Saratoga, Albany, and down the Hudson (by rail or boat) to New York, or *vice versa.*

First class $29.10

ROUTE 990.—NEW YORK TO NIAGARA FALLS, OGDENSBURG, OTTAWA, MONTREAL, and return, *via* Erie Railway to Elmira, Binghampton, Buffalo, NIAGARA FALLS, Rochester, Syracuse, Sandy Creek, Ogdensburg, ferry over St. Lawrence River to Prescott, rail to Ottawa, steamer down Ottawa River to Lachine, rail to Montreal, Rouse's Point, Lake Champlain, White Hall, Saratoga, Albany, and down the Hudson (by rail or boat) to New York, or *vice versa.*

First class $36.80

ROUTE 991.—NEW YORK TO NIAGARA FALLS, ALEXANDRIA BAY, and return, *via* Erie Railway to Elmira, Buffalo, NIAGARA FALLS, Rochester, Syracuse, Sandy Creek, Cape Vincent, steamer to ALEXANDRIA BAY, returning to Cape Vincent, rail to Rome, Albany, down the Hudson (by rail or boat) to New York, or *vice versa.*

First class $23.15

ROUTE 992.—NEW YORK TO NIAGARA FALLS, ALEXANDRIA BAY, and return, *via* Hudson River to Albany, rail to Rochester, Syracuse, NIAGARA FALLS, returning to Syracuse, Sandy Creek, Cape Vincent, steamer to ALEXANDRIA BAY, and return to Cape Vincent, rail to Rome, Albany, and down the Hudson to New York, or *vice versa.*

First class $24.00

ROUTE 993.—NEW YORK TO OGDENSBURG, OTTAWA, MONTREAL, and return, *via* Hudson River (rail or boat) to Albany, rail to Rome, Ogdensburg, ferry to Prescott, rail to OTTAWA CITY, steamer down Ottawa River to Lachine, rail to Montreal, Rouse's Point, Lake Champlain, Lake George, Saratoga, Albany, and down the Hudson (by rail or boat) to New York, or *vice versa*.
First class $32.70

ROUTE 994.—NEW YORK TO OTTAWA CITY and return, *via* Hudson River to Albany, rail to Rome, Ogdensburg, ferry over St. Lawrence to Prescott, rail to OTTAWA CITY, and back the same way.
First class $22.90

ROUTE 995.—NEW YORK TO ALEXANDRIA BAY, MONTREAL, and return, *via* Hudson River (rail or boat) to Albany, rail to Rome, Cape Vincent, steamer to Alexandria Bay, Prescott, Rapids of St. Lawrence, MONTREAL, Lachine, steamer on Ottawa River to Ottawa City, rail to Prescott, steamer to Ogdensburg, rail to Rome, Albany, and steamer down the Hudson to New York.
First class $32.20

ROUTE 996.—NEW YORK TO ALEXANDRIA BAY, MONTREAL, and return, *via* Hudson River steamer to Albany, rail to Rome, Cape Vincent, steamer to Alexandria Bay, Rapids of St. Lawrence, MONTREAL, rail to Rouse's Point, steamer on Lake Champlain to Whitehall, rail to Saratoga, Albany, and Hudson River steamer to New York. $27.75
First class $27.75

ROUTE 997.—NEW YORK TO ALEXANDRIA BAY, MONTREAL, BOSTON, and return, *via* Hudson River to Albany, rail to Rome, Cape Vincent, steamer to Alexandria Bay, Rapids of St. Lawrence, Montreal, rail to Portland, rail or boat to Boston, and Fall River line to New York.
First class $31.30

ROUTE 998.—NEW YORK TO ALEXANDRIA BAY, MONTREAL and return, *via* Hudson River (rail or boat) to Albany, rail to Rome, Cape Vincent, steamer to ALEXANDRIA BAY, 1000 Islands, Prescott, rail to Ottawa City, steamer on Ottawa River to Lachine, rail to Montreal, Rouse's Point, steamer to Whitehall, rail to Saratoga, Albany, and boat to New York.
First class $30.10

ROUTE 999.—NEW YORK TO ALEXANDRIA BAY and return, *via* Hudson River (rail or boat) to Albany, Cape Vincent, steamer to ALEXANDRIA BAY, 1000 Islands, Prescott, Ogdensburg, rail to Rome, Albany, and steamer to New York.
First class $21.30

ROUTE 1000.—NEW YORK TO ALEXANDRIA BAY, MONTREAL and return, *via* rail or boat to Albany, rail to Rome, Cape Vincent, steamer to ALEXANDRIA BAY, 1000 Islands, Prescott, rail to Ottawa City, steamer to Lachine, rail to Montreal, Rouse's Point, steamer to Fort Ticonderoga, stage to Lake George, steamer to Caldwell, stage to Glen Falls, rail to Saratoga, Albany, and rail or boat to New York.
First class $32.50

TOURS TO THE ADIRONDACKS, &c.

ROUTE 1001.—NEW YORK TO AU SABLE CHASM and return. *via* Hudson River steamer to Albany, rail to Saratoga, Whitehall, steamer to Plattsburg, rail to AU SABLE STATION stage to CHASM, and return the same way.
First class $20.50

ROUTE 1002.—NEW YORK TO AU SABLE CHASM, ADIRONDACKS and return, *via* Hudson River steamer to Albany, rail to Saratoga, Whitehall,

boat to Port Kent, stage to AU SABLE CHASM, Paul Smith's or Martin's, returning same way to Albany, thence by rail to New York, or *vice versa*.
First class   -   -   -   -   -   -   ;   -   **$25.00**

ROUTE 1002 B.—NEW YORK TO AU SABLE CHASM, ADIRONDACKS
and return, *via* same route as above to Whitehall, thence steamer to Plattsburg,
rail to AU SABLE STATION, stage to Paul Smith's or Martin's, returning same
way.
First class   -   -   -.   -   -   :-   -.   -   ;   **$26.00**

ROUTE 1003.—NEW YORK TO LAKE GEORGE, ADIRONDACKS and
return, *via* Hudson River steamer to Albany, rail to Saratoga, Glen's Falls,
stage to Caldwell, boat on LAKE GEORGE, stage to Ticonderoga, boat to Port
Kent, stage to Au Sable Chasm, Paul Smith's or Martin's, and back to Port
Kent, boat to Whitehall, rail to Saratoga, Albany, New York, or *vice versa*.
First class   -   -   .   -.   -   -   -.   .   -   **$28.95**

ROUTE 1003 B.—NEW YORK TO LAKE GEORGE, ADIRONDACKS and
return, same as route above to Ticonderoga, thence steamer to Plattsburg, rail
to Au Sable Station, Paul Smith's or Martin's, returning same way to Au Sable
Station, thence rail to Plattsburg, steamer to Whitehall, rail to Saratoga, Albany, New York, or *vice versa*.
First class   -   -   -   -   -   -   -   -   **$29.95**

TOURS TO NIAGARA FALLS, 1000 ISLANDS, RAPIDS OF ST. LAWRENCE, MONTREAL, QUEBEC, LAKE GEORGE, LAKE CHAMPLAIN, BOSTON, &c.

ROUTE 1004.—NEW YORK TO KINGSTON, *via* Hudson River steamer to
Albany, and rail to Niagara Falls, or *via* Erie or N. Y. Central Railroad, all
rail to Niagara, thence rail to Toronto, *via* Hamilton and Suspension Bridge,
and boat on Lake Ontario to Kingston.
First class **$17.55**

ROUTE 1005.—NEW YORK TO PRESCOTT, *via* Erie or N. Y. Central
Railroad to Buffalo, or *via* Hudson River steamer to Albany, rail to Niagara
Falls, rail or boat to Toronto, rail or boat to Prescott.
First class **$20.25**

ROUTE 106.—NEW YORK TO OGDENSBURG, *via* N. Y. Central or Erie
Railroad to Buffalo, or Hudson River steamer to Albany, Niagara Falls, rail or
boat to Toronto, Kingston, Prescott, omnibus and ferry to Ogdensburg.
First class **$20.25**

ROUTE 1007.—NEW YORK TO OTTAWA CITY, *via* Hudson River to
Albany, rail to Syracuse, Niagara Falls, Hamilton, Toronto, steamer on Lake
Ontario, 1000 Islands, Prescott, rail to Ottawa.
First class **$21.80**

ROUTE 1008.—NEW YORK TO OGDENSBURG and return, *via* Hudson
River day or night boat to Albany, Syracuse, Niagara Falls, Hamilton, Toronto, steamer on Lake Ontario to Kingston, 1000 Islands, Prescott, Ogdensburg,
rail to Rome, Albany, and down the Hudson to New York.
First class **$29.70**

ROUTE 1009.—NEW YORK TO MONTREAL, *via* Hudson River to Albany,
rail to Niagara Falls, Hamilton, Toronto, steamer on Lake Ontario, 1000 Islands,
Prescott, rail to Ottawa City, and steamer down Ottawa River to Lachine and
Montreal.
First class   .   .   .   :   .   .   **$27.50**

ROUTE 1010.—NEW YORK TO MONTREAL, *via* Hudson River (rail or
steamer) to Albany and Troy, rail to Saratoga, Schenectady, Rochester, Niagara

Falls, Suspension Bridge, Hamilton, Toronto, rail or boat to Kingston, Prescott, passing 1000 Islands and Rapids of St. Lawrence.

First class $25.05

ROUTE 1011.—NEW YORK TO MONTREAL, *via* Erie or N. Y. Central Railroad to Buffalo, Niagara Falls, Suspension Bridge, Hamilton, Toronto, rail or boat to Kingston, Prescott, passing 1000 Islands and Rapids of St. Lawrence.

First class $23.25

ROUTE 1012.—NEW YORK TO MONTREAL AND QUEBEC, *via* Hudson River to Albany, thence rail to Niagara Falls, or *via* Erie or N. Y. Central Railroad, all rail to Buffalo and Niagara Falls, Suspension Bridge, Hamilton, Toronto, boat on Lake Ontario to Kingston, Prescott, 1000 Islands, Montreal, QUEBEC.

First class $25.75

ROUTE 1013.—NEW YORK TO MONTREAL AND QUEBEC, *via* Hudson River steamer to Albany rail to Troy, Saratoga, Whitehall, steamer to Rouse's Point, rail to Montreal and QUEBEC.

First class $17.00

ROUTE 1014.—NEW YORK TO MONTREAL AND QUEBEC, *via* Hudson River to Albany, rail to Syracuse, Rochester, Niagara Falls, Toronto, steamer on Lake Ontario to 1000 Islands, Prescott, rail to Ottawa City, and steamer down the Ottawa River to Lachine, Montreal, and rail to Quebec.

First class $33.95

ROUTE 1015.—NEW YORK TO QUEBEC AND PORTLAND, *via* Hudson River steamer to Albany and Troy, rail to Saratoga, Rochester, Niagara Falls, Suspension Bridge, Hamilton, Toronto, boat or rail to Kingston, Prescott, 1000 Islands, Rapids of St. Lawrence, Montreal, Quebec, rail to PORTLAND.

First class $35.05

ROUTE 1016.—NEW YORK TO BOSTON, *via* Hudson River steamers to Albany and Troy, Saratoga, Rochester, Niagara Falls, Suspension Bridge, Hamilton, Toronto, boat on Lake Ontario to Kingston, Prescott, 1000 Islands, Rapids of St. Lawrence, Montreal, Quebec, rail to Portland, BOSTON.

First class $36.70

ROUTE 1017.—NEW YORK TO BOSTON, *via* Hudson River (rail or boat) to Albany, rail to Niagara Falls, Toronto, boat to Kingston, Prescott, 1000 Islands, Rapids of St. Lawrence, Montreal, boat or rail to Quebec, rail to Portland and BOSTON.

First class . . . . . , $34.90

ROUTE 1018.—NEW YORK TO BOSTON, *via* Hudson River steamer to Albany or Troy, rail to Saratoga, Rochester, Niagara Falls, Suspension Bridge, Hamilton, Toronto, boat or rail to Kingston, Prescott, 1000 Islands, Rapids of St. Lawrence, Montreal, rail to Portland and Boston.

First class $32.05

ROUTE 1019.—NEW YORK TO BOSTON, *via* Hudson River to Albany, rail to Syracuse, Rochester, Niagara Falls, Hamilton, Toronto, steamer on Lake Ontario, 1000 Islands, Rapids of St. Lawrence, Montreal, St. Johns, Newport, White River Junction, Nashua, Concord, BOSTON.

First class $31.15

ROUTE 1020.—NEW YORK TO QUEBEC AND BOSTON, *via* same route as above to Montreal, thence by rail or boat to QUEBEC, rail to Portland and Boston.

First class . . . . . . $33.

ROUTE 1021.—NEW YORK TO QUEBEC AND BOSTON, *via* Hudson River to Albany, rail to Syracuse, Rochester, Niagara Falls, Hamilton, Toronto, steamer on Lake Ontario, 1000 Islands, Rapids of St. Lawrence, Montreal,

rail or boat to QUEBEC, rail to Sherbrooke, Newport (Lake Memphremagog), White River Junction, Nashua, Concord, BOSTON.
First class $35.15

ROUTE 1022.—NEW YORK TO SARATOGA SPRINGS, *via* steamer on Hudson River to Albany, thence rail to Niagara Falls, Suspension Bridge, Hamilton, Toronto, rail or boat to Kingston, Prescott, 1000 Islands, Rapids of St. Lawrence, Montreal, rail to Rouse's Point, steamer to Fort Ticonderoga, stage to Lake George, steamer to Caldwell, stage to Glen's Falls, and rail to SARATOGA SPRINGS.
First class $32.65

ROUTE 1023.—NEW YORK TO SARATOGA SPRINGS, *via* Erie or New York Central Railroad to Buffalo, or Niagara Falls, or boat on Hudson to Albany, and rail to Niagara Falls, rail or boat to Toronto, Kingston, Prescott, 1000 Islands, Rapids of St. Lawrence, Montreal, rail to Rouse's Point, Whitehall, and SARATOGA SPRINGS.
First class $34.25

ROUTE 1024.—NEW YORK TO MONTREAL and return, *via* Erie or New York Central Railroad to Buffalo, Niagara Falls, Suspension Bridge, Hamilton, Toronto, boat or rail to Kingston, Prescott, 1000 Islands, Rapids of St. Lawrence, MONTREAL, rail to Rouse's Point, steamer on Lake Champlain to Fort Ticonderoga, stage to Lake George, steamer to Caldwell, stage to Glen's Falls, rail to Saratoga, Albany, and steamer down Hudson to New York,
First class $37.05

ROUTE 1025.—NEW YORK TO MONTREAL and return, *via* Erie or New York Central Railroad to Buffalo and Niagara Falls, Suspension Bridge, Hamilton, Toronto, rail or boat to Kingston, Prescott, 1000 Islands, Rapids of St. Lawrence, Montreal, rail to Rouse's Point, steamer on Lake Champlain to Whitehall, rail to Saratoga, Albany, and steamer down Hudson to New York.
First class $34.00

ROUTE 1026.—NEW YORK TO MONTREAL, BOSTON, and return, *via* Hudson River steamer to Albany and Troy, rail to Saratoga, Rochester, Niagara Falls, Suspension Bridge, Hamilton, Toronto, rail or boat to Kingston, Prescott, 1000 Islands, Rapids of St. Lawrence, MONTREAL, rail to Portland, BOSTON, Newport, or Fall River, and steamer on Long Island Sound to New York.
First class $38.10

ROUTE 1027.—NEW YORK TO MONTREAL, BOSTON, and return, *via* Erie or New York Central Railroad, rail to Buffalo and Niagara Falls, or steamer up Hudson to Albany, thence rail to Niagara Falls, Lewiston, boat to Toronto, and same as route above to New York.
First class $36.30

ROUTE 1028.—NEW YORK TO MONTREAL, QUEBEC, BOSTON, and return, *via* Hudson River steamer to Albany, rail to Schenectady, Rochester, Niagara Falls, Suspension Bridge, Hamilton, Toronto, rail or boat to Kingston, Prescott, 1000 Islands, Rapids of St. Lawrence, MONTREAL, Quebec, Portland, BOSTON, Newport, or Fall River, and boat on Long Island Sound to New York.
First class $38.20

ROUTE 1029.—NEW YORK TO MONTREAL, QUEBEC, BOSTON, and return, *via* Erie or New York Central Railroad to Buffalo and Niagara Falls, rail or boat to Toronto, and same as above to New York.
First class $39.30

ROUTE 1030.—NEW YORK TO MONTREAL, SARATOGA, AND BOSTON, *via* Erie or New York Central Railroad to Buffalo and Niagara Falls, rail or boat to Toronto, Kingston, Prescott, 1000 Islands, Rapids of St. Lawrence, MONTREAL, rail to Rouse's Point, steamer on Lake Champlain to Whitehall, rail to SARATOGA, Rutland, Bellows Falls, Fitchburg, BOSTON.
First class $36.25

ROUTE 1031.—NEW YORK TO MONTREAL, SARATOGA, BOSTON, and return, same as above to Boston, thence rail to Newport or Fall River, and steamer on Long Island Sound to New York.
First class $40.65

ROUTE 1032.—NEW YORK TO MONTREAL, SARATOGA, BOSTON, and return, *via* Hudson River to Albany, rail to Niagara Falls, Hamilton, Toronto, steamer on Lake Ontario, 1000 Islands, Rapids of St. Lawrence, MONTREAL, Rouse's Point, Lake Champlain, SARATOGA, Schenectady, Albany, Springfield, BOSTON, Fall River or Newport, and Sound steamer to New York.
First class $41.25

ROUTE 1033.—NEW YORK, NIAGARA FALLS, MONTREAL, and return, *via* Hudson River steamer to Albany, rail to Rochester and NIAGARA FALLS, rail or boat to Toronto, Kingston, Prescott, 1000 Islands, Rapids of St. Lawrence, MONTREAL, rail to Sherbrooke, White River Junction, South Vernon, Springfield, Newhaven, Hartford, New York.
First class $33.15

ROUTE 1034.—NEW YORK, NIAGARA FALLS, MONTREAL, QUEBEC, and return, *via* Hudson River steamer or rail to Albany, Rochester, Niagara Falls, Suspension Bridge, Hamilton, Toronto, rail or boat to Kingston, Prescott, 1000 Islands, MONTREAL, QUEBEC, rail to Sherbrooke, White River Junction, South Vernon, Springfield, New Haven, Hartford, New York.
First class $36.15

ROUTE 1035.—NEW YORK, NIAGARA FALLS, MONTREAL, QUEBEC, and return, *via* New York Central or Erie Railroad to Buffalo and Niagara Falls, rail or boat to Toronto, Kingston, Prescott, 1000 Islands, MONTREAL, QUEBEC, and same as above back to New York.
First class $37.25

ROUTE 1036.—NEW YORK, NIAGARA FALLS, MONTREAL, BOSTON, and return, same as above to MONTREAL, thence rail to Sherbrooke, White River Junction, Concord, Nashua, BOSTON, Newport or Fall River, and by Sound steamer back to New York.
First class $36.65

ROUTE 1037.—NEW YORK, NIAGARA FALLS, MONTREAL, QUEBEC, BOSTON, and return, *via* Hudson River steamer to Albany, rail to Rochester, NIAGARA FALLS, Suspension Bridge, Hamilton, Toronto, rail or boat to Prescott, 1000 Islands, MONTREAL, QUEBEC, rail to Sherbrooke, White River Junction, Concord, Nashua, BOSTON, Newport or Fall River, and Sound steamer back to New York.
First class $39.55

COMBINING WHITE MOUNTAINS.

ROUTE 1038.—NEW YORK TO MONTREAL, QUEBEC, WHITE MOUN-TAINS AND BOSTON and return, *via* Erie or Hudson River Railroad to Buffalo and Niagara Falls, or steamer up the Hudson to Albany, thence rail to Niagara Falls, rail or steamer to Toronto, Kingston, Prescott, 1000 Islands, Rapids of St. Lawrence, MONTREAL, Quebec, rail to Sherbrooke, Wells River, Littleton, stage to Profile House and Bethlehem, rail to Fabyan House, stages to Crawford House, and base of Mountain, Tip Top House by Mount Washington Railway, stages to Glen House, Gorham, rail to Portland and Boston, Fall River Line to New York.
First class $62.65

ROUTE 1039.—NEW YORK TO MONTREAL, WHITE MOUNTAINS, AND BOSTON and return, *via* Hudson River steamer to Albany and Troy, rail to Saratoga, Rochester, Niagara Falls, Suspension Bridge, Hamilton, Toronto, rail or boat to Kingston, Prescott, 1000 Islands, Rapids of St. Lawrence, MONTREAL,

rail to St. John3, White River Junction, Wells River, Littleton, stage to Profile House and Bethlehem, rail to Fabyan House, stages to Crawford House and back, rail to Concord, Nashua, BOSTON, and Fall River Line to New York.
First class $52.95

ROUTE 1040.—NEW YORK, MONTREAL, QUEBEC, WHITE MOUNT-AINS, BOSTON, and return, *via* Erie or New York Central Railroad to Buffalo and Niagara Falls, or *via* steamer on Hudson to Albany, and rail to Niagara Falls, Suspension Bridge, Hamilton, Toronto, rail or boat to MON-TREAL, *via* 1000 Islands, QUEBEC, rail to Sherbrooke, Newport, Wells River, Littleton, stage to Profile House and Bethlehem, rail to Fabyan House, stage to Crawford House and back, rail to Concord, Nashua, Boston, Fall River or New-port, and steamer to New York.
First class $63.65

ROUTE 1041.—NEW YORK, NIAGARA FALLS, MONTREAL, WHITE MOUNTAINS, and return, *via* Hudson River steamer to Albany, rail to Roch-ester, NIAGARA FALLS, rail or boat to Toronto, Prescott, 1000 Islands, Mon-treal, Gorham, stages to Glen House and Summit, rail to base of Mountain, stage to Fabyan House, rail to Bethlehem, stages to Profile House and Littleton, rail to Concord, Nashua, BOSTON, Fall River or Newport, and Sound steamer to New York.
First class $52.55

ROUTE 1042.—NEW YORK, NIAGARA FALLS, MONTREAL, WHITE MOUNTAINS, and return, *via* Erie or New York Central Railroads, or steamer on Hudson to Albany, Niagara Falls, Hamilton, Toronto, steamer on Lake On-tario, 1000 Islands, Rapids of St. Lawrence, MONTREAL, Northumberland, Fabyan House, Bethlehem, stages to Profile House and Littleton, rail to Con-cord, Nashua, Worcester, Allyn's Point, and steamer to New York.
First class $44.25

ROUTE 1043.—NEW YORK, NIAGARA FALLS, MONTREAL, WHITE MOUNTAINS, and return, *via* Erie Railway or Hudson River (rail or boat) to Albany, rail to Niagara Falls, Hamilton, Toronto, steamer on Lake Ontario, 1000 Islands, Rapids of St. Lawrence, MONTREAL, Northumberland, Fabyan House, Bethlehem, stages to Profile House and Littleton, rail to Concord, Nashua, West Concord, Mansfield, Weir Junction, Newport, and Sound steamer to New York.
First class $44.25

ROUTE 1044.—NEW YORK, NIAGARA FALLS, MONTREAL, WHITE MOUNTAINS, and return, *via* Hudson River (rail or boat) to Albany, and rail to Niagara Falls, or rail direct by Erie Railway, Hamilton, Toronto, steamer on Lake Ontario, 1000 Islands, Rapids of St. Lawrence, MONTREAL, Northumber-land, Concord, Nashua, Lowell, Mansfield, Weir Junction, Fall River, Newport, and Sound steamer to New York.
First class $38.75

ROUTE 1045.—NEW YORK TO NIAGARA FALLS, MONTREAL, WHITE MOUNTAINS, SARATOGA, and return, *via* Erie Railway to Niagara Falls, Hamilton, Toronto, steamer to 1000 Islands, Rapids of St. Lawrence, MON-TREAL, Gorham, stages to Glen House and Tip Top House, rail to base of Mountain, stage to Fabyan House, rail to Bethlehem, stage to Profile House and Littleton, rail to White River Junction, Burlington, steamer on Lake Cham-plain to Fort Ticonderoga, stage to Lake George, steamer to Caldwell, stage to Glen Falls, rail to Saratoga, Albany, and steamer down Hudson to New York.
First class $63.30

ROUTE 1046.—QUEBEC TO CACOUNA and return, *via* steamer or Grand Trunk Railway to Riviere du Loup, and stage to Cacouna, returning the same way. To be used in connection with tickets to Quebec.
First class $3.00

ROUTE 1047.—QUEBEC TO TADOUSAC and return, *via* Grand Trunk Railway, or steamer *Magnet* and *Union* to Riviere du Loup and Tadousac, returning same way. To be used in connection with tickets to Quebec.
First class $7.50

ROUTE 1048.—QUEBEC TO HA HA BAY and return, *via* Grand Trunk Railway, or steamer *Magnet* or *Union* to Riviere du Loup and Ha Ha Bay, returning same way. To be used in connection with Quebec tickets.
First class $9.00

Tours to Niagara, Montreal, Gulf of St. Lawrence, Nova Scotia, Halifax, &c.

ROUTE 1050.—NEW YORK TO NIAGARA, QUEBEC, GULF OF ST. LAWRENCE, NOVA SCOTIA and return, *via* Erie or New York Central Railway, or Hudson River day or night boat to Albany, NIAGARA FALLS, Hamilton, Toronto, steamer on Lake Ontario to 1000 Islands, Montreal, QUEBEC, steamer down Gulf of St. Lawrence to Point du Chene, rail to Moncton, St. John, Bangor, Portland, Boston, Fall River, or Newport and Sound steamer to New York.
First class - - - - . . . - $54.25

ROUTE 1051.—NEW YORK TO NIAGARA, QUEBEC, NOVA SCOTIA and return, *via* Hudson River (rail or boat), to Albany, NIAGARA FALLS (or by Erie Railway direct), Hamilton, Toronto, steamer to 1000 Islands, Montreal, QUEBEC, steamer down St. Lawrence and through the Gulf of St. Lawrence to Point du Chene, rail to Halifax, Annapolis, steamer across the Bay of Funday to St. John, and rail to Frederickton Junction, Bangor, Portland, Boston, Fall River or Newport, and Sound steamer to New York.
First class - - - - - - - - $61.85

ROUTE 1052.—NEW YORK TO NIAGARA, QUEBEC, NOVA SCOTIA and return, *via* Erie or New York Central (or boat to Albany), Niagara Falls, Toronto, 1000 Islands, Montreal, QUEBEC, steamer down St. Lawrence River and Gulf of St. Lawrence to Point Du Chene, rail to Halifax, Moncton, St. John, steamer to Portland, and rail to Boston, Fall River or Newport, and Sound steamer to New York.
First class - - - - - - - - $59.35

ROUTE 1053.—NEW YORK TO NIAGARA, QUEBEC, NOVA SCOTIA and return, *via* Erie or New York Central R. R. (or boat to Albany), to Niagara Falls, Toronto, 1000 Islands, Montreal, QUEBEC, steamer on St. Lawrence and Gulf of St. Lawrence to Point Du Chene, rail to St. John, and steamer to Portland, rail to Boston, Fall River or Newport, and Sound steamer to New York.
First class - - - - - - - - $50.45

ROUTE 1054.—NEW YORK TO NIAGARA, QUEBEC, NOVA SCOTIA and return, *via* Erie or New York Central R. R. (or boat to Albany), to Niagara Falls, Toronto, 1000 Islands, Montreal, QUEBEC, steamer on St. Lawrence and Gulf to Point Du Chene, rail to Halifax, Annapolis, steamer across Bay of Funday to St. John, rail to Portland, steamer to Boston, and rail to Fall River, Newport, and steamer to New York.
First class - - - - - - - - $61.45

ROUTE 1055.—NEW YORK TO NIAGARA, QUEBEC, NOVA SCOTIA and return, same as above to QUEBEC, steamer down St. Lawrence and on Gulf of St. Lawrence to Shediac, Pictou, rail to Moncton, St. John, Bangor, Portland, Boston, Fall River, Newport, and steamer on Sound to New York.
First class - - - - - - - - $58.65

ROUTE 1056.—NEW YORK TO NIAGARA, QUEBEC, NOVA SCOTIA and return, *via* Erie or New York Central R. R. (or boat to Albany), to Niagara Falls, Toronto, 1000 Islands, Montreal, QUEBEC, steamer on St. Lawrence River and Gulf to Shediac, Pictou, rail to Truro, St. John, steamer to Portland, rail to Boston, Fall River, Newport, and steamer to New York.

First class - - - - - - - - - $53.85

ROUTE 1057.—NEW YORK TO NIAGARA, QUEBEC, NOVA SCOTIA and return, same as above to QUEBEC, thence steamer on River and Gulf of St. Lawrence to Shediac, Pictou, rail to Truro, St. John, Bangor, Portland, steamer to Boston, rail to Fall River, Newport, and Sound steamer to New York.

First class - - - - - - - - - $58.25

ROUTE 1058.—NEW YORK TO NIAGARA, QUEBEC, NOVA SCOTIA and return, *via* Erie or New York Central R. R. (or boat to Albany), to Niagara Falls, Toronto, 1000 Islands, Montreal, QUEBEC, steamer on River and Gulf of St. Lawrence to Shediac, Pictou, rail to Truro, St. John, and steamer to Portland, Boston, rail to Fall River, Newport, and Sound steamer to New York.

First class - - - - - - - - - $53.85

ROUTE 1059.—NEW YORK TO NIAGARA, QUEBEC, NOVA SCOTIA and return, *via* same as above to QUEBEC, steamer on River and Gulf of St. Lawrence to Shediac, Pictou, rail to Halifax, Annapolis, steamer on Bay of Funday to St. John, rail to Bangor, Portland, Boston, Fall River, Newport, and Sound steamer to New York.

First class - - - - - - - - - $60.85

ROUTE 1060.—NEW YORK TO NIAGARA, QUEBEC, NOVA SCOTIA and return, *via* Erie or New York Central R. R. (or boat to Albany), to Niagara Falls, Toronto, 1000 Islands, Montreal, QUEBEC, steamer on River and Gulf of St. Lawrence to Shediac, Pictou, rail to Halifax, Annapolis, steamer across Bay of Funday to St. John, Portland, rail to Boston, Fall River or Newport, and Sound steamer to New York.

First class - - - - - - - - - $56.05

ROUTE 1061.—NEW YORK TO NIAGARA, QUEBEC, NOVA SCOTIA and return, same as above to QUEBEC, steamer on Gulf and River St. Lawrence to Pictou, rail to Halifax, Annapolis, steamer across Bay of Funday to St. John, Portland and Boston, rail to Fall River, Newport, and Sound steamer to New York.

First class - - - - - - - - - $55.40

ROUTE 1062.—NEW YORK TO NIAGARA, QUEBEC, NOVA SCOTIA and return, *via* Erie or New York Central R. R. (or boat to Albany), Niagara Falls, Toronto, 1000 Islands, Montreal, QUEBEC, steamer on River and Gulf of St. Lawrence to Shediac, Pictou, rail to Halifax, Moncton, St. John, Bangor, Portland, rail or boat to Boston, Fall River, Newport, and Sound steamer to New York.

First class - - - - - - - - - $62.15

ROUTE 1063.—NEW YORK TO NIAGARA, QUEBEC, NOVA SCOTIA and return, same as above to QUEBEC, thence steamer down St. Lawrence and Gulf of St. Lawrence to Pictou, rail to Halifax, Moncton, St. John, steamer to Portland, rail to Boston, Fall River, Newport, and Sound steamer to New York.

First class - - - - - - - - - $57.35

ROUTE 1064.—NEW YORK TO NIAGARA, QUEBEC, NOVA SCOTIA and return, *via* Erie or New York Central R. R. (or boat to Albany), NIAGARA, Toronto, steamer on Lake Ontario to 1000 Islands, Montreal, QUEBEC, steamer on River and Gulf of St. Lawrence to Shediac, Point Du Chene, rail to Halifax, steamer to Portland, rail or boat to Boston, rail to Fall River, Newport, and Sound steamer to New York.

First class - - • • • • • • • $53.05

Tours to Boston, Montreal, Quebec, Nova Scotia, Mount Desert, Lake Champlain, Lake George, Saratoga, Hudson River, Newport, White Mountains, &c., &c.

ROUTE 1065.—NEW YORK TO MOUNT DESERT and return, *via* Fall River steamer to Newport, Fall River, rail to Boston, rail or boat to Portland, boat to South West Harbor (MT. DESERT), and return the same way.

First class - - - - - - - - - $18.70

ROUTE 1066.—NEW YORK TO MOUNT DESERT and return, *via* Fall River Line to Newport and Boston, rail or boat to Portland, steamer to Bar Harbor (MT. DESERT), and return the same way.

First class - - - - - - - - - $20.90

ROUTE 1067.—NEW YORK TO MOUNT DESERT and return, *via* Fall River Line to Newport and Boston, rail or boat to Portland, steamer to South West Harbor (MT. DESERT), returning same way to Portland, rail or boat to Boston, rail to Worcester, Springfield, Albany, and by boat down the Hudson to New York, or *vice versa*.

First class - - - - - - - - - $22.05

ROUTE 1068.—NEW YORK TO MT. DESERT and return, *via* Fall River line to Newport and Boston, rail or boat to Portland, steamer to Bar Harbor (MT. DESERT), returning same way to Portland, rail or boat to Boston, rail to Worcester, Springfield, Albany, and steamer down the Hudson to New York, or *vice versa*.

First class $24.25

ROUTE 1069.—NEW YORK TO FREDERICKTON, ST. JOHN and return, *via* Fall River Line to Boston, rail or boat to Portland, rail to Bangor, FREDERICKTON, steamer down the St. John River to St. John, steamer to Portland, rail to Boston, Fall River Line to New York, or *vice versa*.

First class $27.90

ROUTE 1070.—NEW YORK TO ST. JOHN, FREDERICKTON and return, *via* Fall River Line to Boston, steamer to Portland, ST. JOHN, steamer on St. John River to Frederickton, rail to Bangor, Portland, Boston, and Fall River Line back to New York, or *vice versa*.

First class $27.25

ROUTE 1071.—NEW YORK TO MT. KINEO (Moosehead Lake) and return, *via* Fall River Line to Boston, rail to Portland, Bangor, Guilford, stage to Greenville, boat on Moosehead Lake to MT. KINEO, and return the same way.

First class $36.60

ROUTE 1072.—NEW YORK TO MT. KINEO (Moosehead Lake) and return, *via* Fall River Line to Boston, rail or boat to Portland, rail to Dexter, stage to Greenville, and boat on Lake to MT. KINEO, returning same way.

First class $28.10

ROUTE 1073.—NEW YORK TO MT. KINEO and return, *via* Fall River Line to Boston, boat to Bangor, rail to Dexter, stage to Greenville, and boat to MT. KINEO, returning same way.

First class $29.50

ROUTE 1074.—NEW YORK TO ST. JOHN and return, *via* Fall River line to Newport and Boston, rail or boat to Portland, boat to ST. JOHN, rail to Bangor, down the Kenebec River to Portland, rail to Boston, and Fall River line to New York, or *vice versa*.

First class $24.80

ROUTE 1075.—NEW YORK TO ST. JOHN and return, *via* Fall River line to Newport and Boston, rail or boat to Portland, boat to St. John, rail to Bangor, Portland, Boston, and Fall River line to New York, or *vice versa*.

First class $25.90

ROUTE 1076.—NEW YORK TO ST. JOHN and return, *via* Fall River line to Boston, steamer to St. John, and return to New York same way.

First class $19.80

ROUTE 1077.—NEW YORK TO ST. JOHN and return, *via* Fall River line to Boston, rail to Portland, and boat to St. John, returning same way.

First class $21.10

ROUTE 1078.—NEW YORK TO ST. JOHN and return, *via* Fall River line to Newport and Boston, rail to Portland, Bangor, St. John, returning same way.

First class $30.70

ROUTE 1079.—NEW YORK TO HALIFAX and return, *via* Fall River line to Newport and Boston, rail or boat to Portland, rail to Bangor, St. John, steamer across Bay of Fundy to Annapolis, rail to HALIFAX, and return same way to New York.

First class $40.70

ROUTE 1080.—NEW YORK TO HALIFAX and return, *via* Fall River line to Newport and Boston, rail or boat to Portland, rail to Bangor, St. John, Moncton, Truro, HALIFAX, and return same way to New York.

First class $43.30

ROUTE 1081.—NEW YORK TO HALIFAX and return, *via* Fall River line to Boston, rail or boat to Portland, rail to Bangor, St. John, Moncton, Truro, HALIFAX, Annapolis, steamer across Bay of Fundy to St. John, rail to Bangor, steamer to Portland, rail to Boston, Fall River, Newport, and steamer to New York, or *vice versa*.

First class $40.90

ROUTE 1082.—NEW YORK TO HALIFAX and return, *via* Fall River line to Boston, rail or boat to Portland, steamer to HALIFAX, rail to Annapolis, steamer to St. John, Portland, rail to Boston, and back by Fall River line to New York, or *vice versa*.

First class $27.10

ROUTE 1083.—NEW YORK TO HALIFAX and return, *via* Fall River line to Newport and Boston, rail to Portland, steamer to HALIFAX, and back same way to New York.

First class $23.10

ROUTE 1084.—NEW YORK TO NOVA SCOTIA, QUEBEC, and return, *via* Fall River line to Boston, rail or boat to Portland, rail to Bangor, St. John, Point du Chene, steamer on Gulf and River St. Lawrence to QUEBEC, rail to Portland, rail or boat to Boston, rail to Fall River, Newport, and steamer to New York, or *vice versa*.

First class $45.90

ROUTE 1085.—NEW YORK TO ST. JOHN, NOVA SCOTIA, QUEBEC, and return, *via* Fall River line to Boston, rail or boat to Portland, steamer to Bangor, rail to St. John, Point du Chene, steamer on Gulf and River St. Lawrence to QUEBEC, rail to Portland, steamer or rail to Boston, Fall River line to New York, or *vice versa*.

First class $44.80

ROUTE 1086.—NEW YORK TO ST. JOHN, NOVA SCOTIA, QUEBEC, and return, *via* Fall River line to Boston, rail or boat to Portland, steamer to St. John, rail to Point du Chene, steamer on Gulf and River St. Lawrence to QUEBEC, rail to Portland, rail or boat to Boston, and Fall River line to New York, or *vice versa*.

First class $41.10

ROUTE 1087.—NEW YORK TO ST. JOHN, HALIFAX, NOVA SCOTIA, QUEBEC, and return, *via* Fall River line to Boston, rail or boat to Portland, rail to Bangor, St. John, steamer across Bay of Fundy to Annapolis, rail to Halifax, Truro, Pictou, steamer on Gulf and River St. Lawrence to Quebec, rail to Portland, rail or boat to Boston, and Fall River line to New York, or *vice versa.*
First class	.	.	.	.	.	$52.50

ROUTE 1088.—NEW YORK TO ST. JOHN, HALIFAX, NOVA SCOTIA, QUEBEC, and return, *via* Fall Line to Boston, boat or rail to Portland, steamer to Bangor, rail to ST. JOHN, steamer to Annapolis, rail to Halifax, Pictou, steamer to Quebec, rail to Portland, rail or boat to Boston, and Fall River line to New York, or *vice versa.*
First class	.	.	.	.	$51.35

ROUTE 1089.—NEW YORK TO HALIFAX, NOVA SCOTIA, QUEBEC, and return, *via* Fall River line to Boston, rail to Portland, boat to HALIFAX, rail to Pictou, boat to QUEBEC, rail to Portland, rail or boat to Boston, and Fall River line to New York, or *vice versa.*
First class	.	.	.	.	$43.60

ROUTE 1090.—NEW YORK TO MONTREAL, QUEBEC, NOVA SCOTIA, and return, *via* Hudson River (rail or boat), to Albany, Saratoga, White Hall, boat on Lake Champlain to Rouse's Point, rail to MONTREAL, QUEBEC, and steamer on River and Gulf of St. Lawrence to Point du Chene, rail to St. John, Bangor, Portland, rail or boat to Boston, Fall River line to New York, or *vice versa.*
First class	.	.	.	.	.	$47.20

ROUTE 1091.—NEW YORK TO MONTREAL, QUEBEC, NOVA SCOTIA, and return, *via* Hudson River (rail or boat) to Albany, rail to Saratoga, Glen Falls, Stage to Caldwell, steamer on Lake George, stage to Fort Ticonderoga, steamer to Rouse's Point, rail to MONTREAL, QUEBEC, steamer on River and Gulf of St. Lawrence to Point du Chene, rail to St. John, Bangor, Portland, rail or boat to Boston, and Fall River line to New York, or *vice versa.*
First class	.	.	.	.	$49.60

ROUTE 1092.—NEW YORK TO QUEBEC, NOVA SCOTIA and return, *via* Hudson River to Albany, Saratoga, Lake Champlain, Rouses Point, Montreal, QUEBEC, steamer on River and Gulf of St. Lawrence to Point du Chene, rail to St. John, steamer to Portland, rail to Boston, and Fall River Line to New York, or *vice versa.*
First class	.	.	.	.	$41.60

ROUTE 1093.—NEW YORK TO QUEBEC, NOVA SCOTIA and return, *via* Hudson River to Albany, rail to Saratoga, steamer on Lake Champlain to Rouses Point, rail to Montreal, QUEBEC, steamer on River and Gulf of St. Lawrence to Point du Chene, Pictou, rail to Halifax, Annapolis, steamer on Bay of Fundy to St. John, rail to Bangor, Portland, rail or boat to Boston, and Fall River Line to New York, or *vice versa.*
First class	.	.	.	$43.90

ROUTE 1094.—NEW YORK TO QUEBEC, NOVA SCOTIA and return, *via* Hudson River (rail or boat) to Albany, rail to Saratoga, steamer on Lake Champlain, Rouse's Point, rail to Montreal, QUEBEC, steamer to Point du Chene, Pictou, rail to Halifax, Annapolis, steamer to St. John, Portland, rail to Boston and Fall River, steamer to New York, or *vice versa.*
First class	.	.	.	.	.	$46.60

ROUTE 1095.—NEW YORK TO QUEBEC, NOVA SCOTIA and return, *via* same route as above to Halifax, from thence by steamer to Portland and rail to Boston, and Fall River Line to New York, or *vice versa.*
First class	.	.	.	.	$42.50

Tours to Prince Edward's Island.

ROUTE 1096.—NEW YORK TO CHARLOTTESTOWN and return, *via* Fall River Line to Boston, rail or boat to Portland, rail to Bangor, St. John, Moncton, Shediac, and steamer to CHARLOTTESTOWN, returning same way.

First class $42.70

ROUTE 1097.—NEW YORK TO CHARLOTTESTOWN and return, *via* Fall River Line to Boston, rail or boat to Portland, boat to St. John, rail to Shediac, steamer to CHARLOTTESTOWN, returning same way.

First class $33.10

ROUTE 1098.—NEW YORK TO CHARLOTTESTOWN and return, *via* Fall River Line to Boston, rail or boat to Portland, rail to Bangor, St. John, Shediac, and boat to CHARLOTTESTOWN, returning to Shediac, rail to St. John, and steamer to Portland, rail or boat to Boston, Fall River Line to New York, or *vice versa*.

First class $37.90

ROUTE 1099.—NEW YORK TO CHARLOTTESTOWN and return, *via* Fall River Line to Boston, rail or boat to Portland, rail to Bangor, St. John, steamer on Bay of Fundy to Annapolis, rail to Halifax, Pictou, steamer to CHARLOTTESTOWN, and return the same way.

First class $51.10

ROUTE 1100.—NEW YORK TO CHARLOTTESTOWN and return, *via* Fall River Line to Boston, rail or boat to Portland, rail to Bangor, St. John, Moncton, Halifax, Pictou, steamer to CHARLOTTESTOWN, returning by steamer to Shediac, rail to St. John, steamer to Portland, rail to Boston, and Fall River Line to New York, or *vice versa*.

First class $43.40

ROUTE 1101.—NEW YORK TO CHARLOTTESTOWN and return, *via* Fall River Line to Boston, rail or boat to Portland, steamer to Halifax, rail to Pictou, boat to CHARLOTTESTOWN, boat to Shediac, rail to St. John, Bangor, Portland, Boston, and Fall River Line to New York, or *vice versa*.

First class $38.10

ROUTE 1102.—NEW YORK TO CHARLOTTESTOWN and return, *via* Fall River Line to Boston, rail or boat to Portland, rail to Bangor, St. John, steamer on Bay of Fundy to Annapolis, rail to Halifax, Pictou, steamer to CHARLOTTESTOWN, steamer to Shediac, rail to St. John, Bangor, Portland, Boston, and back to New York.

First class $46.90

ROUTE 1103.—NEW YORK TO CHARLOTTESTOWN and return, *via* Fall River Line to Boston, boat or rail to Portland, steamer to St. John, Annapolis, rail to Halifax, Pictou, steamer to CHARLOTTESTOWN, steamer to Shediac, rail to Moncton, St. John, Bangor, Portland, Boston, and Fall River Line, back to New York, or *vice versa*.

First class $42.10

ROUTE 1104.—NEW YORK TO HAWKESBURY and return, *via* Fall River Line to Boston, rail or boat to Portland, rail to Bangor, St. John, boat to Annapolis, rail to Halifax, Pictou, boat to HAWKESBURY, returning by boat to Pictou, rail to Truro, Moncton, St. John, boat to Portland, rail to Boston, and Fall River Line to New York, or *vice versa*.

First class $47.70

ROUTE 1105.—NEW YORK TO HAWKESBURY and return, *via* Fall River Line to Boston, rail or boat to Portland, steamer direct to Halifax, rail to Pictou, boat to HAWKESBURY, returning by boat to Pictou, rail to Halifax, Annapolis, boat to St. John, rail to Bangor, Portland, Boston and Fall River Line to New York, or *vice versa*.

First class $44.60

TOURS TO QUEBEC, BOSTON, WHITE MOUNTAINS, &c.

ROUTE 1106.—NEW YORK TO QUEBEC and return, *via* steamer to New London, rail to White River Junction, Newport (Lake Memphrenagog), Sherbrooke, Quebec, and back by the same route.

First class $25.40

ROUTE 1107.—NEW YORK TO QUEBEC and return, *via* rail to New Haven, Springfield, Newport, Sherbrooke, QUEBEC, Sherbrooke, Littleton, stage to Profile House, Crawford House, Bethlehem, rail to Wells' River, Springfield, New York.

First class $37.70

ROUTE 1108.—NEW YORK TO QUEBEC and return, *via* rail to New Haven, Springfield, Newport, Sherbrooke, QUEBEC, returning same way.

First class $26.70

ROUTE 1109.—NEW YORK TO QUEBEC and return, *via* rail to New Haven, Springfield, Newport, Sherbrooke, QUEBEC, Wells' River, Littleton, stage to Profile House, Crawford House, North Conway, Centre Harbor, Lake Winnipiseogee, steamer to Weir's, rail to Concord. Nashua, Boston, and Fall River Line to New York.

First class $41.50

ROUTE 1110.—NEW YORK TO QUEBEC and return, same as above to QUEBEC, thence rail to Gorham, stage to Glen House, Conway, and Centre Harbor, steamer to Alton Bay, rail to Boston, and Fall River Line to New York, or *vice versa*.

First class $37.20

ROUTE 1111.—NEW YORK TO QUEBEC and return, *via* rail to New Haven, Springfield, Sherbrooke, QUEBEC, Gorham, stage to Glen House, North Conway, rail to Portland, Boston, and Fall River Line to New Yord, or *vice versa*.

First class $35.50

ROUTE 1112.—NEW YORK TO QUEBEC and return, same as above to QUEBEC, thence steamer to Montreal, rail to St. John's, White River Junction, Concord, Nashua, Boston, and Fall River Line to New York. or *vice versa*.

First class $31.80

ROUTE 1113.—NEW YORK TO QUEBEC and return, *via* rail to New Haven, Springfield, Newport (Lake Mephremagog), Sherbrooke, QUEBEC, steamer to Montreal, rail to Rouse's Point, steamer to Fort Ticonderoga, stage and boat on Lake George to Caldwell, stage to Glen's Falls, rail to Saratoga, Albany, and steamer down the Hudson to New York, or *vice versa*.

First class $28.70

ROUTE 1114.—NEW YORK TO QUEBEC and return, *via* rail to New Haven, Springfield, Wells' River, Littleton, stage to Profile House, Crawford House, Bethlehem, rail to Wells' River, Newport (Lake Memphremagog), Sherbrooke, QUEBEC, steamer to Montreal, rail to Rouse's Point, steamer to Whitehall, rail to Saratoga, Troy, and New York, or *vice versa*.

First class $39.30

ROUTE 1115.—NEW YORK TO LAKE CHAMPLAIN, MONTREAL, QUEBEC, BOSTON and return, *via* Hudson River (rail or boat) to Albany, rail to Troy, Saratoga steamer on Lake Champlain to Rouse's Point, rail to Montreal, steamer on St. Lawrence to QUEBEC, and back to Montreal, rail to St. John, Newport, White River Junction, Concord, Nashua, Boston, Fall River or Newport, and Sound steamer to New York, or *vice versa*.

First class $32.60

ROUTE 1116.—NEW YORK TO LAKE GEORGE, QUEBEC, MONTREAL, BOSTON, and return, *via* Hudson River (rail or boat), to Albany,

Saratoga, Glen Falls, stage to Lake George, steamer on Lake, and stage to Fort
Ticonderago, steamer on Lake Champlain to Rouse's Point,.rail to Montreal,
steamer to QUEBEC and back to Montreal, rail to Newport, White River Junction, Concord, Nashua, Boston, and Fall River steamers to New York, or *vice
versa.*
First class $35.60

TOURS TO THE WHITE MOUNTAINS,
GOING AND RETURNING VIA BOSTON.

ROUTE 1117.—NEW YORK TO NORTH CONWAY and return, *via* Fall
River Line to Boston, rail to Wolfboro, NORTH CONWAY, and back the same
way.
First class $19.80
ROUTE 1118.—NEW YORK TO NORTH CONWAY and return, *via* Fall
River Line to Boston, rail to Portland, NORTH CONWAY and back the same way.
First class $18.10
ROUTE 1119.—NEW YORK TO NORTH CONWAY and return, *via* Fall
River Line to Boston, rail to Portland, NORTH CONWAY, and back by rail to
Wolfboro, Boston, Fall River Line to New York.
First class $18.95
ROUTE 1120.—NEW YORK TO CRAWFORD HOUSE and return, *via*
Fall River Line to Boston, rail to Portland, North Conway, Bemis' stage to
CRAWFORD HOUSE, Fabyan House, Base of Mountain, stage to Summit, and
return same way to North Conway, thence rail to Wolfboro, Boston, Fall River
Line to New York, or *vice versa.*
First class $32.55
ROUTE 1121.—NEW YORK TO WHITE MOUNTAINS and return, *via*
Fall River Line to Boston, rail to Concord, Plymouth, Wells' River, Fabyan
House, stage to Crawford House, Bemis', rail to North Conway, Portland, Bos-
ton, and Fall River Line to New York, or *vice versa.*
First class $24.30
ROUTE 1122.—NEW YORK TO WHITE MOUNTAINS and return, *via*
Fall River Line to Boston, rail to Lowell, Nashua, Concord, Plymouth, Wells'
River, Littleton, Fabyan House, stage to Crawford House, Bemis', North Con-
way, Wolfboro, Boston, and Fall River Line back to New York, or *vice versa.*
First class $24.80
ROUTE 1123.—NEW YORK TO WHITE MOUNTAINS and return, same
as above to Littleton, stage to Profile House, Bethlehem, rail to Fabyan House,
stage to Crawford House, Bemis', rail to North Conway, Portland, Boston, and
Fall River Line back to New York, or *vice versa.*
First class $28.55
ROUTE 1124.—NEW YORK TO WHITE MOUNTAINS and return, *via*
Fall River Line to Boston, rail to Lowell, Nashua, Concord, Plymouth, Wells'
River, Littleton, Fabyan House, stage to Base of Mt. Washington, rail to Sum-
mit, return same way to Fabyan House, stage to Crawford House, Bemis', rail
to North Conway, Portland, Boston, and Fall River Line to New York, or *vice
versa.*
First class $35.55
ROUTE 1125.—NEW YORK TO WHITE MOUNTAINS and return, *via*
Fall River Line to Boston, rail to Lowell, Nashua, Concord, Plymouth, Wells'
River, Fabyan House, stage to Base of Mountain, rail to Summit, stage to Glen
House, North Conway, rail to Wolfboro, Boston and Fall River Line back to
New York, or *vice versa.*
First class .   .   . $33.30

ROUTE 1126.—NEW YORK TO WHITE MOUNTAINS and return, *via* same as above to North Conway, thence rail to Portland, Boston, aud Fall River Line back to New York, or *vice versa*.

First class $34.80

ROUTE 1127.—NEW YORK TO WHITE MOUNTAINS and return, *via* Fall River Line to Boston, rail to Lowell, Nashua, Concord, Plymouth, Wells' River, Littleton, stage to Profile House, Bethlehem, rail to Fabyan House, stage to Base Mt. Washington, rail to Summit, stage to Glen House, North Conway, rail to Portland, Boston, and Fall River Line back to New York, or *vice versa*.

First class - - - - - - - - - $37.00

ROUTE 1128.—NEW YORK TO WHITE MOUNTAINS and return, *via* Fall River Line to Boston, rail to Lowell, Nashua, Concord, Plymouth, stage to Profile House, Bethlehem, rail to Fabyan House, stage to Crawford House. Bemis, rail to North Conway, Portland, Boston, and Fall River Line to New York, or *vice versa*.

First class - - - - - - - - $28.20

ROUTE 1129.—NEW YORK TO WHITE MOUNTAINS and return, *via* same route as above to Fabyan House, stage to Base of Mt. Washington, stage to Summit, and back same way to Fabyan House, stage to Crawford House, Bemis', rail to North Conway, Portland, Boston, and Fall River Line to New York, or *vice versa*.

First class - - - - - - - - - $35.20

ROUTE 1130.—NEW YORK TO WHITE MOUNTAINS and return, *via* Fall River Line to Boston, rail to Lowell, Nashua, Concord, Plymouth, stage to Profile House, Bethlehem, rail to Fabyan House, stage Base of Mt. Washington, rail to Summit, stage to Glen House, North Conway, rail to Portland, Boston, and by Fall River Line to New York, or *vice versa*.

First class - - - - - - - - $36.80

ROUTE 1131.—NEW YORK TO WHITE MOUNTAINS and return, *via* Fall River Line to Boston, rail to Portland, Gorham, stage to Glen House, Summit of Mt. Washington, rail to Base, stage to Fabyan House, Crawford House, Bemis', rail to North Conway, Wolfboro, Boston, and Fall River Line to New York.

First class - - - - - - - - $33.80

ROUTE 1132.—NEW YORK TO WHITE MOUNTAINS and return, *via* Fall River Line to Boston, rail to Portland, Gorham, stage to Glen House, Summit of Mt. Washington, rail to Base, stage to Fabyan House, rail to Littleton, Wells' River, Plymouth, Concord, Lowell, Boston, and Fall River Line to New York.

First class - - - - - - - - $33.80

ROUTE 1133.—NEW YORK TO WHITE MOUNTAINS and return, *via* same route as above to Glen House, thence stage through Pinkham Notch to Glen Station, rail to Bemis', stage to Crawford House, Fabyan House, rail to Wells' River, Plymouth, Concord, Lowell, Boston, and Fall River Line to New York.

First class - - - - - - - - $29.00

ROUTE 1134.—NEW YORK TO WHITE MOUNTAINS and return, *via* Fall River Line to Boston, rail to Portland, Gorham, stage to Glen House, Summit of Mt. Washington, rail to Base, stage to Fabyan House, Crawford House, Bemis', rail to North Conway, Wolfboro, Boston, and Fall River Line to New York.

First class - - - - - - - - $29.55

ROUTE 1135.—NEW YORK TO WHITE MOUNTAINS and return, *via* Fall River Line to Boston, rail to Lowell, Concord, Plymouth, stage to Profile

House, Littleton, rail to Wells' River, Plymouth, Concord, Boston, and Fall River Line back to New York.

First class - - - - - - - - - $25.45

ROUTE 1136.—NEW YORK TO WHITE MOUNTAINS and return, *via* Fall River Line to Boston, rail to Alton Bay, steamer on Lake Winnepesaukie to Centre Harbor, Weir's, rail to Plymouth, stage Profile House, Littleton, rail to Wells River, Plymouth, Concord, Nashua, Boston, and Fall River Line to New York, or *vice versa*.

First class - - - - - - - - - $00.00

ROUTE 1137.—NEW YORK TO WHITE MOUNTAINS and return, *via* Fall River Line to Boston, rail to Portland, North Conway, Bemis' stage to Crawford House, Fabyan House, rail to Wells' River, Plymouth, Weirs, Steamer on Lake Winnepesaukie to Centre Harbor, Alton Bay rail to Boston, and Fall River Line to New York, or *vice versa*.

First class - - - - - - - - - $00.00

TOURS TO WHITE MOUNTAINS VIA LAKE CHAMPLAIN.

ROUTE 1138.—NEW YORK TO WHITE MOUNTAINS and return, *via* Hudson River (rail or boat) to Albany, rail to Troy, Saratoga, Whitehall, Rouse's Point, Montreal, St John, Newport (Lake Memphremagog), Wells' River, Littleton, Fabyan House, stage to Crawford House, Base of Mt. Washington, rail to Summit, stage to Glen House, North Conway, rail to Portland, Boston, and Fall River Line to New York, or *vice versa*.

First class - - - - - - - - - $41.00

ROUTE 1139.—NEW YORK TO WHITE MOUNTAINS and return, *via* Hudson River (rail or boat) to Albany, rail to Troy, Saratoga, Glen's Falls, stage to Caldwell, boat on Lake George, stage to Fort Ticonderoga, boat to Rouse's Point, rail to Montreal, St. John's, Newport (Lake Memphremagog), Wells' River, Littleton, Fabyan House, stage to Base of Mt. Washington, rail to Summit, back same way to Fabyan House, stage to Crawford House, Bemis', rail to North Conway, Portland, Boston, and Fall River Line to New York, or *vice versa*.

First class - - - - - - - - - $44.75

ROUTE 1140.—NEW YORK TO WHITE MOUNTAINS and return, *via* Hudson River (rail or boat) to Albany, rail to Saratoga, Whitehall, boat to Rouse's Point, rail to Montreal, St. John, Newport, (Lake Memphremagog), Wells' River, Littleton, stage to Profile House, Bethlehem, rail to Fabyan House, stage to Crawford House, Bemis', rail to North Conway, Portland Boston, and Fall River Line to New York, or *vice versa*.

First class - - - - - - - - - $34.55

ROUTE 1141.—NEW YORK TO WHITE MOUNTAINS and return, *via* Hudson River (rail or boat), to Albany, rail to Saratoga, Glen's Falls, stage to Caldwell, boat on Lake George, stage to Fort Ticonderoga, boat to Rouse's Point, rail to Montreal, St. John, Newport, (Lake Memphremagog), Wells' River, Littleton, stage to Profile House, Bethlehem, rail to Fabyan House, stage to Crawford House, Bemis', rail to North Conway, Portland, Boston, and Fall River Line to New York, or *vice versa*.

First class - - - - - - - - - $37.95.

ROUTE 1142.—NEW YORK TO WHITE MOUNTAINS and return, *via* Hudson River (rail or boat) to Albany, rail to Saratoga, Whitehall, boat to Rouse's Point, Montreal, St. John's, Newport, (Lake Memphremagog,) Wells' River, Plymouth, stage to Profile House, Bethlehem, rail to Fabyan House, stage to Base of Mt. Washington, rail to Summit, stage to Glen House, North Conway, Portland, Boston, and Fall River Line to New York, or *vice versa*.

First class - - - - - - - - - $42.70

ROUTE 1143.—NEW YORK TO WHITE MOUNTAINS and return, *via* same route as above to North Conway, thence rail to Wolfboro, Boston, and Fall River Line back to New York, or *vice versa*.

First class - - - - - - - - - - $43.20

ROUTE 1144.—NEW YORK TO WHITE MOUNTAINS and return, *via* Hudson River (rail or boat) to Albany, rail to Saratoga, Glen's Falls, stage to Caldwell, boat on Lake George, stage to Fort Ticonderoga, boat to Rouse's Point, rail to Montreal, St. John's, Newport, (Lake Memphremagog,) Wells' River, Plymouth, stage to Profile House. Bethlehem, rail to Fabyan House, stage to Base of Mt. Washington, rail to Summit, stage to Glen House, North Conway, Wolfboro, Boston, and Fall River Line to New York, or *vice versa*.

First class - - - - - - - - - $46.75

ROUTE 1145.—NEW YORK TO WHITE MOUNTAINS and return, *via* same route as above to North Conway, thence rail to Portland, Boston, and Fall River Line to New York, or *vice versa*.

First class - - - - - - - - - $46.25

INFORMATION FOR PASSENGERS
HOLDING
Cook's American Tourist Tickets,
TIME OF STEAMBOAT DEPARTURES AND ARRIVALS.

Quebec and Gulf Ports.

S. S. GEORGIA leaves Quebec every Friday, 7 1 M.
    Arrive Shediac (Point du Chene), every Monday, 2 A. M.
      "   Pictou,   "   "   7 P. M.
S. S. SECRET & MIRAMICHI leaves Quebec every Tuesday, 2 P. M.
    Arrive Shediac (Point du Chene), every Saturday, 2 A. M.
      "   Pictou,   "   "   1 P. M.
    Leaves Pictou,   "   Monday, 7 P. M.
      "   Shediac (Point du Chene),   "   Tuesday, 5 P. M.
    Arrives Quebec,   "   Saturday, 10 A. M.
S. S. GEORGIA leaves Pictou, every Friday, 12:50 P. M.
    "   Shediac (Point du Chene), every Saturday, 5 A. M.
    Arrives Quebec,   "   Monday, 11   "

Bay of Fundy Steamers.

The "Empress" or "Scud" leaves Reed's Wharf, St. John, daily, at 8 A. M., and connects at Annapolis with Express train to Halifax. Leave Annapolis, daily, on arrival of trains from Halifax, at 2:15 P. M., arriving at St. John, at 8 P. M., connecting with trains on European and North American Railway, and International S. S. Co.

New England and Nova Scotia S. S. Co

Steamer FALMOUTH leaves Portland for Halifax, every Saturday, at 5.30 P. M.
    "   Halifax for Portland,   "   Tuesday, at 4 P. M.

Portland, Bangor & Machias Steamboat Co

Steamer LEWISTON leaves Portland every Tuesday and Friday evening at 10 o'clock (touching from June 25th to Sept. 19th, at Bar Harbor, for Mt. Desert.)

Steamer CITY OF RICHMOND leaves Portland for Bangor, every Monday, Wednesday and Friday evenings, at 10 o'clock, arriving at 10 o'clock following morning. Leaves Bangor on every Monday, Wednesday and Friday mornings, at 6 o'clock.

International Steamship Co.

For Portland, Eastport and St. John.

Steamers depart as follows : In April, May, June, October, November and December.

Leave Boston every Monday and Thursday at 8 A. M.
" Portland " " " at 6 P. M.
In July, August and September.
Leave Boston every Monday, Wednesday and Friday, at 8 A. M.
" Portland " " " " at 6 P. M.
Steamers leave St. John, same days as from Portland and Boston.

Saguenay River Line.

Steamers SAGUENAY, ST. LAWRENCE, UNION, from June 20th till September 10th, leave Quebec, daily (except Sunday and Monday), on arrival of Montreal boat.

Portland Steam Packet Co.

Steamers JOHN BROOKS & FOREST CITY leave Boston, from India Wharf, daily, except Sunday, at 7 P. M.
Leave Portland, from Franklin Wharf, at 7 P. M.

Hudson River Day Boats.

Steamer C. VIBBARD and DANIEL DREW leave Pier 41 North River, foot of Vestry Street, New York, every morning, except Sunday, at 8:30 o'clock. Leave foot of 23rd Street, 15 minutes later.

Hudson River Night Boats.

ST. JOHN and DREW leave Pier 40, North River, foot of Canal Street, every evening, except Sunday, at 6 o'clock.

Fall River Line.

Steamers BRISTOL and PROVIDENCE leave Pier 28, North River, daily, at 5 P. M.

Canadian Navigation Company.

Steamer CITY OF TORONTO leaves Lewiston, daily, at 11 A. M., for Toronto.
Steamers leave Toronto, daily, Sundays excepted, at 2 P. M., for 1,000 Islands, Rapids of St. Lawrence and Montreal; reach Montreal at 7 P. M. the next day.
Steamers leave Canal Basin, Montreal, at 9 o'clock every morning, except Sunday, and Lachine, on the arrival of the noon train ; these steamers pass through the Canal, and do not run the Rapids on the trip from Montreal.

Steamers on St. John River

Leave St. John for Frederickton, daily, at 9 A. M.
" Frederickton for St. John " " 9 A. M.

Richelieu Steamers

Leave Montreal for Quebec, daily, at 7 P. M.
" Quebec for Montreal, " at 4 P. M.

Lake Champlain Steamers

Leave Rouse's Point for White Hall, daily, at 8 A. M., and 5:55 P.M.
" White Hall for Rouse's Point, daily, at 10:45 A. M. and 8:20 P. M.

Collingwood Line, Lake Superior.

Leave Collingwood every   at   P. M.
"   Sault St. Marie every
Arrive Thunder Bay every
"   Duluth every
Leave Duluth every
"   Thunder Bay every
"   Sault St. Marie every
Arrive Collingwood every

Western Transportation Co. and Anchor Line,

BETWEEN BUFFALO AND CHICAGO.

STEAMERS

Fountain City,	*China*,	*Empire State*,
India,	*Idaho*,	*Eowhaw*
Badger State,	*Japan*,	*Oneida*,

leave Buffalo every evening, except Sundays and Mondays, at 7 P. M.
Tuesdays, Thursdays and Saturdays steamers leave foot of Washington St.
Wednesdays and Fridays steamers leave foot of Evans street. No boats Friday, July 3d, 17th, 31st, August 14th and 28th, and September 11th.

Steamers between Sandusky, Put in Bay and Detroit.

MEALS AND BERTHS INCLUDED.

Steamer JAY COOKE leaves Detroit at 8:40 A. M.
"   Put in Bay at 1:00 P. M.
"   Kelley's Island at 2:00 P. M.
arrive Sandusky 3:00 P. M.
leave Sandusky 6:30 P. M.
"   Put in Bay 8:00 P. M.
arrive Detroit 12:30 A. M.

St. Louis and New Orleans and Merchants' Southern Packet Line.

INCLUDING MEALS AND STATEROOM.

BETWEEN NEW ORLEANS AND ST. LOUIS.

One of the following first class steamboats

Great Republic,	*Tom Jasper*,	*Pauline Carroll*,
John Kyle,	*City of Quincy*,	*Susie Silver*,
City of Alton,	*James Howard*,	*Richmond*,
Bismarck,	*John A. Scudder*,	*Commonwealth*,
Glencoe,	*Henry Ames*,	

leave St. Louis and New Orleans daily.

Keokuk Northern Line Packet Co.

One of the following Steamers

Leave St. Louis, daily, at 12 noon.
"   St. Paul,   "   "   6 P. M.

Andy Johnson,	*Alex. Mitchell*,	*Red Wing*,
Rob Roy,	*Clinton*,	*Belle of La Crosse*,
Minneapolis,	*Northwestern*,	*J. H. Johnson*,
Lake Superior,	*Dubuque*,	*Minnesota*.

www.ingramcontent.com/pod-product-compliance
Lightning Source LLC
Chambersburg PA
CBHW021527090426
42739CB00007B/813